R.E. BEING SERVED?

Successful Strategy and Tactics for the School R.E. Department

by
Terence Copley

CIO PUBLISHING
Church House, Dean's Yard, London SW1P 3NZ

ISBN 0 7151 9033 4

Published 1985 for the General Synod Board of Education by
CIO Publishing

About the Author

Terence Copley is at present Deputy Head and a teacher in the R.E.
Department at the Ecclesbourne School, Duffield, Derby, a co-
educational comprehensive school. He has previously been Senior Lec-
turer in R.E. at the College of Ripon and York St. John; Director of the
Sixth Form at Westwood High School, Leek, Staffs.; and Head of R.E.
at Hinchingbrooke School, Huntingdon, another co-educational comprehensive.

He is co-author of *A Bedside Book For R.E. Teachers* and *First School R.E.*
(SCM Press), and has edited *In The Beginning*, published by the
National Society's York R.E. Centre, for probationer teachers of R.E.
He is a regular contributor to the *British Journal of Religious Education*.

Printed in Great Britain by Spottiswoode Ballantyne Printers Ltd.,
Colchester and London

Contents

Foreword

This is a handbook about survival and victory. The testing-ground is the uncharted terrain of a school R.E. Department. Our author, Terence Copley, is well-known for his pungent examination, in previous books, of the aims and methods of R.E. Now, however, he gives us something entirely different: a manual on practical day-to-day strategy and tactics, written with a unique combination of enthusiasm and the know-how that only years of experience can provide.

How do you organise timetabling, class and homework marking, meetings with colleagues? Cope with staff changes and personality clashes inside the department? Get the best out of all available resources, human and otherwise? Handle interviews effectively? Arrange successful visits? Ensure that your administration runs like clockwork while your teaching keeps the children's interest alive? Just read on . . .

The book is written from the perspective of the County Secondary School R.E. Department, with separate sections dealing with the specialist areas of R.E. in the Church and Primary School. It will, we are confident, appeal to a wide readership: specialist and non-specialist R.E. teachers and those still in training; teachers of other subjects (for much of Mr Copley's advice holds good whatever the department); and those parish clergy and governors who feel the need of a clear picture of a school's administrative workings.

Pamela Egan
Publications Officer
General Synod Board of Education

The Intention of this Book

The theory of R.E. and its place within the curriculum are now relatively well documented. A spate of books for teachers and pupils in the last ten years or so, along with new Agreed Syllabuses, has helped what used to be called the new R.E. out of infancy and towards maturity. This book does not intend to duplicate that coverage. Rather the concern here is with the skill or craft or politics of running R.E. in a school, whether for the sole teacher in charge, or for the head of a department of several, or for those aspiring to such work. In a comprehensive school the R.E. department may number as many as six or seven, when you include those teaching the subject as second string or minority subject; other schools may have the lone specialist; primary schools may not even have that. There may simply be a non-specialist co-ordinator of R.E. in the school.

The aim of this book is to help teachers to use their opportunities to the full to run lively departments; to advance the cause of R.E. in the school; to cut unnecessary corners in departmental organisation; to get R.E. into the top subject charts; to consider some issues that are inessential to curriculum theory but vital to the prosperity of R.E. within a specific school situation.

B.Ed., and Post-Graduate Cert. Ed. courses can claim to teach students to begin to teach R.E. They do not have the time or brief to prepare them to be heads of R.E. later in their teaching lives. Yet some anticipation of such a role may spare them costly mistakes that could impede the progress of the subject in their own school. For aspiring department heads I have tried to pinpoint some of the potential pitfalls.

The section headings in the Contents can be used as a checklist for departmental practice in any school – not as a yardstick of claimed or assumed perfection in practice, but simply as against someone else's approach to the matter. As teachers we are too often reluctant to put

1

ourselves at risk by exposing our practice to the hard-boiled gaze, as we ruefully imagine it, of other colleagues. I have risked it here.

Throughout this book I have made certain assumptions about the nature of R.E.: that it should be open-ended, that it should be concerned with religion as a wide phenomenon as well as giving proper place to Christian studies, and that the classroom is not the proper place for evangelistic activity; moreover, that the teacher must keep his own religious persona under control and in the background. Because this is not a book about the philosophy or methodology of R.E., I have not sought to justify these assumptions. Moderate as they seem to me, I realize that not all readers will share them, especially the last one.

I would make two points about them, however, both important: first, that I do not believe they will render the book worthless or unusable to those who do not share them and, second, that these assumptions are mine alone. They do not express any official view of CIO Publishing, the Board of Education or any other working group with whom I have links. 'Here I stand' – but there is no reason why anyone else should!

A. The Department Meeting

Unless the department is a one man band needing no help even from second-subject R.E. teachers, or unless the head of R.E. arrogates to himself the Fuehrer image, the department meeting should be central to the health of R.E. in the school because, whatever the varied theological training, specialist interests, religious commitments and educational theories of those who teach R.E., they will all agree on one fundamental aim of the whole exercise: children should learn about religion *and* enjoy it.

It is a mistake to assume that the achievement of this aim is as simple as one teacher doing his own thing with a class. The department meeting can be a forum where all can share the strengths of each. It should not threaten staff but strengthen them, department head included, by providing a chance for them to be briefed on routine administrative matters, e.g., arrangements for visits, visiting speakers or report deadlines; for co-ordinating such matters as 'where we all are on the syllabus this week', and for initiating more fundamental discussion on what we are doing, what we should be doing and why. 'How do *you* tackle the Resurrection?' has a very important place in the proceedings. 'Any Other Business' must allow time for members, department head included, to ask for help. No department can be truly integrated in which the confidence to ask for help does not exist, nor the human resources to provide it.

Experience suggests that a weekly blocked meeting on the timetable provides the best opportunity to get together. This avoids the rush of lunch-hour and the jadedness of 4 p.m., while the dictates of time mean that it cannot easily degenerate into a talking shop.

Major policy discussion is best left for the occasional (termly?) evening meeting at the home of one of the department, where one arrives refreshed after tea at home and some relaxation. With evening meetings, the most enthusiastic head of department must remember that by

3

9.30 p.m. most colleagues have had enough and by 10 p.m. they may snore audibly.

The sort of major topics suitable for evening meetings might include:

Setting v. mixed ability in R.E. (assuming the department had a choice);
At what point to separate GCE/CSE pupils;
Exam option recruitment and whether it is working in R.E.;
A common system for department internal assessment – or whether it is desirable;
A major syllabus proposal and review for one Year-group in the school.

The justification for the department meeting and its corollary, consensus government with the department head as team leader, is not simply that it accords with modern thinking but that it works effectively and fairly, and can be a source of support for all concerned. This includes probationer(s), department head, 'minority' R.E. teachers, students on teaching practice, etc.

When the decisions reached affect a wider group than just the department staff, it is useful to minute them formally. The circulation of such minutes can sometimes forewarn senior colleagues of contentious issues and enlist their support. Such issues might include the possible showing of a controversial film in a lesson, the invitation to a 'one-sided' group or visitor in circumstances which prevent the other side coming, the repeated failure of the Deputy Head (Curriculum) despite promises to provide increased time per week for classes, the reasons for the department's requesting its own video recorder and playback system, the department's view on its place within Sixth Form General Studies, or the proposed latest up–dated, fully comprehensive, integrated, syncopated, correlated sex–education course. In a two–person department, meetings may be ad hoc but still merit minutes. Even the one man band may gain from the occasional use of the formal memo to the Head and interested senior staff.

Whether the department is large or small, a Five Year Plan is still essential. It is hard to find a serious title for such an important document. While 'Five Year Plan' has associations for some with USSR plans to increase grain production, 'Manifesto', 'White Paper', etc., carry other unfortunate connotations. I stick to Five Year Plan because it means a plan for five years!

A Five-Year Plan for R.E. in a school can be an asset not only in the department but to the school's headteacher. It should be set out in something like the following format (always typed and with several copies, preferably in a ring binder or spiral-bound):

1. Proposals for syllabus (internal)
2. Proposals for syllabus (external examination courses)
3. Necessary resources (include books, film, video, cost of visitors' expenses)
4. Necessary environment (rooms, storage, display facilities)
5. Staffing implications.

In the first two sections a clear statement needs to be made how changes will be phased in and at what year, and where they depend absolutely on new resources. A year-by-year list of priorities, phasing in appropriately, has to be provided in the third section: a list of all the resources you would need in an ideal situation will help neither the person who draws it up (he doesn't get it) nor the recipient – he is left to discriminate the importance of the items on it, and in such circumstances will invariably follow the non-specialist rule-of-thumb line: buy the three cheapest items!

Section 4 includes blackboards, overhead projectors, reprographic support – again with a clear list of priorities over five years. The chances are that even with falling rolls R.E. will be looking for expansion, for two very valid reasons – its inheritance as a one-time Cinderella subject will not have left it a resource stockpile of goodies to draw on, and the last decade's significant changes in syllabus need new material and have made large quantities of stock unusable.

Similarly it is no use dreaming up ambitious plans for R.E. when there is no hope of staffing them. With falling rolls, the only hope of expanding the R.E. staff may lie in the internal redeployment of someone else within the school to teach some, or more, R.E. This leaves the selection of your new colleague almost to chance (unless the department has cultivated the goodwill of senior staff), and in any well-planned department chance must be minimised. The wrong person can kill the right course and ruin the right resource. Realistic proposals need to be made by the department as to where any extra staff might be found. For example – and this is not untypical: an extra O Level two-year course at

5

4 periods per week will need 8 extra periods. The following options may be available to the school:

(i) R.E. specialist Mrs Y stops teaching second subject English (gains 5 periods for R.E.), and Mr Z who teaches in an over-staffed area (Languages?!), takes on 4 periods of Lower School R.E., releasing 4 more periods of Mrs Y to the new course;

or

(ii) R.E. specialist Mr X contracts out of Sixth Form General Studies (+ 2 periods for R.E.) and Games (+2). The department withdraws from staffing the school's community service project (+4). This covers the extra time needed for the new O Level course;

or

(iii) The department closes a parallel CSE course to the proposed new O Level and finds its eight periods in a straight switch.

Clearly each of these options carries implications and value judgements and clearly it is at department level that the R.E. implications are best understood, so a strong recommendation needs to be made to the senior management member or team who will endorse the proposals. It is better that the department chooses which of the three options it will adopt than that the decision is made above or outside.

A Five-Year written Plan for R.E. can anticipate some of these decisions and their likely consequences. A detailed and carefully-argued written document will obviously take considerable time and consultation to produce. Indeed, such researches into resources, discussion and writing up could easily take two terms, possibly one whole academic year. As the plan nears finalisation it is useful to invite the County R.E. Adviser or, in Church schools, the diocesan Adviser, to join the discussion before any irreversible decisions are reached. The Plan should then be typed and duplicated, with copies for head, senior staff, all the department staff including even one- or two-period per week helpers, and any other interested parties.

Despite the hours involved in its production, I believe there are many advantages to this sort of document:

1. It gives the department a set of clearly defined objectives instead of a term by term muddle and, as the fifth year approaches, a yardstick to measure progress.

6

2. It shows senior staff the direction in which the department is going and in which it intends to go, and that the department is workmanlike in clearly defining its approach.

3. The discussions leading to the Plan are themselves of value to members of the department in establishing areas of agreement and difference, and in establishing priorities for expenditure. The Plan guarantees that the department focuses on long-term aims and objectives as well as on the needs of the moment.

Even in the one-person department these three points largely pertain. In this situation, the discussion with a third party (actually a second party!) – the Adviser – is even more necessary. The written presentation is still very useful for others within the school, especially the head, and in the case of staff change it can help the incoming specialist to appraise the recent history of R.E., and the intended plans for it within the school.

2   CHOOSING A SYLLABUS

No ideal heavenly blueprint, no Platonic Form of the Syllabus exists as a prescription for every department in every situation. It is interesting to note that in recent years even County Agreed Syllabuses have become shorter and shorter on the prescriptive part and longer on the options and hints. Perhaps we are reaching a stage of Darwinian evolution in Agreed Syllabuses in which the fittest will survive as the shortest, most cryptic sentence:

    'R.E. shall be taught!'
or   'Let there be R.E.!'

with a ten-volume handbook to follow on what you might do as R.E.

I shall not enter on the dubious task of attempting to find the lowest common denominator in terms of syllabus content. Any external syllabus, whether examination or Agreed, can be a good servant but a bad master and is no substitute for a department's producing its own, in which R.E. in that school and locality is seen as part of a continuum through primary to secondary schooling, perhaps by way of middle school and perhaps on to 16 to 19 at school or elsewhere. It is possible, however, to provide a checklist against which a department can measure its scheme of work along the following pattern:

Aims
How clear is the department on these?
How do they relate to those of the Agreed Syllabus?
How do they relate to the views of the headteacher, if known?
How do they relate to the governors or diocese in the case of Church schools?
How do they relate to any existing curriculum statement of the LEA?
How does the department intend to transmit them to children, and perhaps their parents, through the total course?

Content
How far does the scheme of work reflect stated aims?
Does it adequately reflect
  (a) the variety of local religious experience and history from pre-Christian times onwards?
  (b) the variety of global religious experience?
  (c) the Christian faith as the major U.K. faith?
  (d) the non-religious approach to experience, so that religion is not presented as the sole option?
  (e) the variety of religious experience within the school population? (In a boarding school or a day school with a far-flung catchment this could differ from (a) above)
  (f) the technical nature of much religious language?

Links
Are you aware of the R.E. in your feeder schools and in schools which your pupils may go on to attend?

Personal, Social, Moral Education
When 'M.E.' figures in R.E. syllabus content without any overt religious point of reference, is the department clear on being able to justify its presence in R.E., and to distinguish it from fudge? Can it justify its time-share in the probably limited time allotted to R.E.?

Balance and Timing
When R.E. and any 'M.E.' content are taken into account, is there an appropriate balance between the two and are they timed to fit suitable

points in the child's development? For example, could a remote rural school in Scotland justify as balanced a syllabus along these lines:

Year 1 Christianity
Year 2 Islam
Year 3 Signs and Symbols
Year 4 Religions of India
Year 5 Moral Issues ?

Consideration of syllabus needs to be linked with consideration of teaching methods. Methods should not simply be the most diverse way of communicating material. They may themselves reflect skills which we need to define and then to try to transmit, e.g.

the ability to argue a case you do not necessarily agree with;
the ability to communicate a religious idea by dance or picture;
the ability to use a Bible;
the ability to listen critically;
the ability to interview someone about their beliefs;
the social skill of appropriate behaviour on visits to places of worship, etc.

A system of trying to define these skills and then to evaluate one's success in transmitting them needs to be built into departmental routines.

Syllabus will always require constant adjustment, evaluation and change, but any major change depends on the ability of the R.E. team to back it with commercial or home-made resources. It is here that the one-person department can find links with departments in nearby schools invaluable, although the Art, Music, English, Dance, Drama and History departments of his own school may well also have material (whether they are using it with children or not) on religious themes which will meet his particular needs. Very special attention needs to be given to the 3rd Year (13+) syllabus, as this is one of the factors that will, or will not, influence options choices for Years 4 and 5 – hence, indirectly, A Level numbers and therefore ultimately the status and future of the department.

In renovating a run-down department where dictates of time and cash prevent the change of all the syllabuses at once, it is best to give priority to Year 1, the first and impressionable year in which success can prevent later hang-ups about R.E.; to Year 3, the year in which options are made; and the Year 4/5 examination course. Zap, pow, kerbam in

Year 1 can create an interest which is hard to extinguish altogether; Year 3 incubates the future of R.E. in the school as a serious subject; a good 4th Year examination course will lead to bigger and more groups in future years.

Nowhere is this attention more vital than in schools which have illegally abandoned general (i.e. non-examination) R.E. in Years 4 and 5. R.E. staff cannot rest content with a situation whereby the R.E. of seven-eighths of the pupils ends at 13 except for a trickle of option candidates. A later task is to strengthen the general R.E. to make it valid and worthwhile – this too can have the bonus of recruiting A Level candidates. Where no such course exists, students who have not followed O Level are much less likely to have the confidence to take the A Level plunge.

3 RESOURCING NEW MATERIAL

Today's ad hoc worksheets can be the basis for tomorrow's lesson and the day after's more carefully phrased offset-litho booklet. Where a team of teachers pool such items, resources can grow relatively cheaply. We are bombarded with commercial material and can afford to buy some; again inter-school loans, which are above-board from a copyright point of view (unless you charge for the loan!), can eke out limited cash and text books which you are not yet sure about buying. A tape slide sequence or video, professionally produced and supported by worksheets of your own, can be highly cost-effective when compared to textbooks, especially paperbacks, since the AVA material can be viewed by hundreds, perhaps thousands of children within its lifetime. A filmstrip or video will go out of date before it wears out; with the textbook the reverse may be the case.

The material most relevant to your own school is self-produced by using the school's video camera, or a borrowed one. Even an audio cassette can have a greater impact than the teacher or class reading a written extract or interview. The self-produced resource, moreover, has the added merit that you can actually involve children in its production. They may, living in today's gadget age, have a technical expertise that their teacher lacks in operating some of the equipment and it is sometimes this sort of activity that can open up R.E. for them as a lively subject. The rule-of-thumb checklist on resources is this:

Has something permanent been added to each Year group each school year? – always accepting that permanence in education is very temporary compared to permanence in religion!

David Sellick in 'Tools of the Trade' (see Acknowledgements) sets out clear and sound advice intended for probationer teachers, but providing good 'revision' for seasoned campaigners:

'The first source is perhaps the most obvious: it is the commercial market. You get hold of these by parting with various-sized chunks of your share of the capitation, so the means is simply "buying". The advantages are that once you've bought it it is there, available, for you to use when you need it. The disadvantages are that, once spent, that money has gone. The second-hand value of 30 4B-soiled textbooks is amazingly low! This suggests that when buying you do really have to be clear about how the item will fulfil your aims. In this matter beware of colleagues' recommendations unless you are absolutely sure that your aims match your colleagues', and that your pupils are similar in age, background and ability. Do get hold of inspection copies, visit Teachers' and R.E. Centres, and call in on College libraries. Try to see some pupils' work following use of the materials, whether it is a textbook, slide set or sound strip.

'The majority of books in R.E. departments will have been bought by your predecessors. Books are most likely to be purchased but perhaps the majority of audio-visual aids used in any single year in a school will be the property of various hire companies. Films, filmstrips, slide sets, artefacts, sound strips, sound tapes and video tapes are the items available for hiring. The advantages are that you get more for your money in any one year compared with buying, and the hire company have the responsibility of keeping the content of the material up-to-date. The disadvantages are that when a point crops up in a lesson you cannot dive into the R.E. stock-room and emerge dressed in a saffron robe complete with begging bowl and needle, nor plug in and switch on the relevant "Everyman" programme. Another disadvantage, especially with films, is the expense involved in pre-viewing. Everybody says this is essential, but it is a strong man who pays the hire fee for a film which was only permitted to be seen by two R.E. teachers who gave it the "thumbs down"! Another problem is the nervous energy lost in wondering whether the items will arrive in time for the lesson. Some teachers regard the fact that they have to book a long time ahead as a disadvantage, but I feel this is rather an advantage because it makes sure that work is planned out well in advance.

'The third type of source is tapped by borrowing materials for free! That is certainly an advantage, but additional disadvantages are that there might be greater pressure on availability because cost-free resources are popular resources and in some cases no income from loan of materials means that the items are not kept as fully up-to-date as those of the hire companies. When the skill of adapting is exercised, the fourth type of source becomes available. In this context adapting demands that one keeps one's eyes open for anything which could be used to assist in the R.E. classroom. This may be resources which colleagues have acquired for their work in other subjects but which could illustrate a point in R.E. The geographer's slide-set on Borneo might have one picture of a religious rite; the historians might have a filmstrip on life in a medieval monastery: the English department may have a moving poem based on a religious experience. But adapting also draws upon what is in the daily newspaper, all sorts of journals and magazines for adults and children. I've used articles from *Woman* and *Jackie*. It is all a matter of being conscious of the possibility of finding particular content to illustrate those concepts everywhere and anywhere in the world which surrounds the R.E. classroom.

'A slight refinement of adapting is making. Here the ingenuity of the adapter is given freer rein. All this is enhanced by the existence in school of an electric stencil-cutting machine. A variety of bits and pieces culled from umpteen sources, given a format and a few well-chosen words, and bingo! A topical, relevant and personal worksheet for 2Y. Actually quite a few commercially produced textbooks for R.E. obviously began life as one teacher's worksheets for his own classes. Quality of reproduction is the problem here; typing is nearly always preferable to handwriting. Pupils do not have the great experience of reading the dozens of near-illegible hands that we do as teachers, and find even our moderately tidy style difficult. It is not only worksheets that can be made; slide-tape programmes, poster-sized photographs, and hand-carved models. But this does bring another disadvantage; if you have spent hours making something and it doesn't go down well with the class it is easy to take the rejection as a personal insult – though maybe your twelve million matchstick model of Solomon's Temple wasn't that good anyway.

'Utilizing people and places in the locality is a sixth type of source. Inviting speakers to talk to classes is more successful with older pupils (15 plus) who have been adequately prepared. Pupils can be taken out to visit places – R.E. field work. The great advantage is authenticity – a real Franciscan Friar with brown habit, three knots and sandals; the actual place where candidates for adult baptism are totally immersed; yes, the water comes out of that tap . . .

'The disadvantages of speakers are that unless you have had him before, you do not know how any visitor will react to pupils (nor vice versa!), and even if you have heard him preach brilliantly to a congregation of a thousand at an evangelical rally, he may undo in one twenty-minute session all that you have slowly been building up for four years.'

The one-person department is at a serious disadvantage with

resources; his capitation allowance is likely to be small and his time is limited. Yet he still has to resource a five-year syllabus, even if there are only three or four forms, not eight or ten, in each year. He needs at the outset to research into:

what can be borrowed from other schools and County Library;
what relevant material can be borrowed from other departments in his school; what topics best lend themselves to co-ordinating children to produce resources which others will use in the future;
whether the resources he chooses to purchase commercially are durable.

4 MARKING AND ASSESSMENT

All subjects, not simply R.E., need clarity in internal marking and assessment. A few schools may enforce a party line on all departments – in which case do not read on in this section! Whatever scheme a department meeting adopts, however, should satisfy three criteria:

1 that the children understand it and it is not perceived as a mystique inside Sir's head;
2 that it takes into account content and presentation;
3 that it is as simple as possible, and avoids the sacred mysteries of B$-$ $-$, C$+$ $+$, 15½/20, etc.

A grid system is one possibility, for instance:

A Excellent work *and* presentation
B Good work *and* presentation
C Average
D Below average in content *or* badly presented *or* part of the work set not completed
E Two or all three of the categories for D fulfilled.

Borderline marks should be kept to an absolute minimum – otherwise we are in practice moving from a five-point to a ten-point scale. Where borderlines do occur they are better indicated as such, e.g., A/B, C/D rather than A$-$, C$-$, etc. The pretence of numerical marks, unless the exercise involves a set of factual answers, is better avoided. Cross-moderation within a department is useful and comparison of marking policy across the humanities subjects can also be helpful. It can, indeed, be vital: I have taught in a school in which R.E. gave marks of C to

13

average work but the History department gave B. This could affect 3rd Year option choices unless the meaning of the grades was clearly understood by the children. That means they have to understand History grading too. However clearly R.E. explains its own grades in this situation, the pupil may be convinced that he is 'better' at History.

Examination courses need to reflect examination standards. This is relatively easy to achieve with timed tests, less easy with course work which forms no part of the eventual exam assessment. To indicate this difference, a different set of grades should perhaps be used; with an A Level group, for instance, timed essays could follow the exam grades A to F when they are marked, whereas for in-term essays – in which the real skills being tested are the abilities to research, analyse and then expound a topic – a grade distinct from test situations, e.g., 1 to 5 or even a three-point scale alpha to gamma, is preferable. The vital point is that the grades must be clear in meaning to the pupils.

It may indeed be preferable on educational grounds to restrict course work to notes far more than is the custom at A Level. Most students are compelled to reduce their course-work essays to notes in order to revise from them, and it seems better practice in the main to concentrate on notes in course work, punctuated by regular test essays under exam conditions. This monitors for the teacher how successfully a topic has been taught, helps the pupils to undertake revision in small and manageable doses and gives that necessary practice in essay technique which is claimed as the benefit of the more traditional homework essay.

The question then arises: should we mark notes? This applies in two areas – examination course notes and non-examination course notes. The two major problems for the R.E. teacher in marking notes are that it takes up an enormous amount of time and is excruciatingly boring. Departments might consider this as a possible solution:

where notes have been set as a result of out-of-lesson research on the part of the pupil, they should be read and, if a mark is necessary, marked on a simple three-point scale that corresponds to Satisfactory, Unsatisfactory and Merit;

where notes have been done in a lesson from a teacher's remarks or from a standard text or work sheet, *a sample only* should be checked by the teacher to ensure that pupils have grasped the topic. A bad sample calls for another sample, and a further bad sample reveals the need for some re-teaching of a topic.

In all this I am making the assumption that no department worthy of its salt will permit *dictated* notes at any level. These are both boring to the children and non–educative. While taking down dictated notes you can be thinking of boy friend/girl friend, football results, what's on TV tonight, anything but the subject in hand. Dictated notes are not worthy of writing, let alone marking.

Frequency of marking is another issue that the department meeting needs to resolve. It is not a productive business for the teacher, yet it is vital to pupil morale, especially in a subject which occupies relatively little timetable space outside exam courses. Again the department needs to standardize if possible, so that a change of R.E. teacher will not lead to a change in marking standards or frequency. I suggest as a possible pattern that normally (a word that is a good escape clause!) in Years 1 to 3 of a comprehensive school, or in all the Years of a middle school, the homework is marked in each form each week. Classwork, unless it is individualized project work, should be sampled as suggested above.

It is interesting at this point to compare the practice of many Maths departments. Maths has the maximum pupil-teacher contact time, with the possible exception of English, and at the same time it is arguably the most mind–blowingly boring subject to mark! Most Maths departments seem to mark homework, but to go over classwork as a whole class and to let the pupils mark their own, raising areas of misunderstanding themselves. (The homework would eventually bring these to Sir's notice anyway, unless Dad has been doing it, in which case the discrepancy with class marks will soon show.)

R.E. is not as different as may at first appear. There is no need to feel guilty about not marking every single piece of written work, especially if it is being sampled. There *is* need for regular marking and for chasing defaulters, but we have a major advantage over the Maths situation, namely that if creative homeworks are being set, every piece is different and therefore less boring to mark. Similarly a homework choice in the lower Years, e.g. illustration, poetry, dramatisation, will lead to more interest from the pupils and more interest for the assessor.

With examination groups, of course, the demand is heavier, both in the length of time needed to assess an individual piece of work and in the length of work. Regularity of marking should match regularity of homework. This will probably be dictated externally; each option pool in Year 4, for instance, may have two homeworks per week. It is useful with exam classes to moderate even course-work marking by passing the occasional batch to a colleague. This can help the class teacher; it can also reduce the rare but real adolescent conviction that Miss Q 'has it in for me and always gives me a bad mark'.

In the case of school internal examinations, some factors – which Years will sit the exams, at what time of year, the maximum length of time for an exam, etc. – will be dictated by school policy, not departmental decision, though there is no reason why the department should not lobby for changes if it feels that they would be helpful. Other factors, however, do come under immediate departmental control. In planning, which should ideally take place before the exams, the department has to decide what content or body of knowledge it wishes to test and what skills it proposes to examine; it must then construct an exam format which takes into account not only these points but also the range of ability of children sitting the exam.

In Years 1 to 3 a common format may help. In an exam set across the whole ability range it might take the following form:

A one hour paper comprising –

20 multi-choice questions: ½ mark each
15 phrase or sentence answers: 1 mark each
3 paragraph answers or answers in five parts (a) to (e) on one topic: 5 marks each
1 imaginative or essay answer: 10 marks.

There are two important and useful questions omitted in this format and it might be necessary to alter the recipe to include one or both of them: one is the *comprehension passage*, which is a long paragraph with ten or more gaps, accompanied by a list of twenty or more words (which include the correct answers and some distractors) for the pupil to insert: a so-called word search. The other, particularly suitable for less able pupils or bottom sets, is a set of *brief questions based on a picture*, e.g. of a Muslim at prayer: Who is this man? What is he doing? How many times each day does he do this? and so on. Experience shows that the less able child can sometimes remember more in recall when stimulated by pictures than by writing. Whatever method is chosen, the format of the exam should be established first of all.

The next task is to prepare a draft paper. The teacher responsible needs several exercise books from each class taught by someone other than himself from which to draft the questions. The draft should then be submitted to each teacher teaching the course, for comment and alteration. From this emerges the paper which the pupils will sit. It is only at this point that a mark scheme should be finalized because, despite all checking procedures, there may be an ambiguity in a question or a class may interpret it in an unpredictable way. Marking is then best undertaken in sections across the whole group rather than in classes or sets, e.g., I mark all the Section A answers in the Year, you do all the Section B, etc. With essay or 'imaginative' answers ('You are a Muslim on Hajj. Describe what you see and what your feelings are') it is desirable to build into the marking a moderation of a sample by a third party.

The department also needs a policy on exam post-mortems. Is there to be a pass mark? In mixed-ability groups should this be different for each child, based on his/her performance during the year? Is there to be a re-examination for some candidates? Are children to do exam corrections? Should pupils who are absent for the exam be made to sit it? Or should they sit a previous year's paper?

There is also the question of 4th Year general, i.e. non-examination, R.E. Of course it would be fatuous to imagine an examination in this along with 'real' exam subjects, based on supposed revision at the end of Year 4. It would, however, be entirely proper to conduct *an assessment*, based largely on skills and including both self-assessment by the pupils and comments on the course, and to conduct this end-of-year assessment in class time, without any revision or warning, just before the school examinations begin. For the pupils it can be a painless way of revision and for the teacher can provide useful feedback on what they have or have not learned. The question of general R.E. continues to be such a vital one that I have included as an appendix (page 78) the syllabus used in the department in which I work and also a copy of the End of Year Assessment relating to it, with notes on how this was conducted and how the syllabus developed. (We withdrew this syllabus in the following July and substituted a new one, also included in the appendix.)

6 BUILDING UP THE O AND A LEVEL GROUPS

Good numbers opting for O and A Level are essential to the health and future of any R.E. department. Moreover they rescue the staff from what can be the fate of hacks, where no exam groups exist, slogging away with a heavy case load and little pupil/teacher contact time. Options in Year 3 are a highly complicated procedure, with pro- and (perhaps more often) anti-R.E. prejudices working in the minds of

17

options advisers, heads of houses, careers staff, parents and pupils. The department meeting needs to give careful thought to how far each of the following factors is operating in its school:

1 *Parental attitudes towards the value of exam R.E.* Has the department produced a leaflet for parents along the lines of the old CEM production 'The New R.E. for Parents'? Do parents know it is a proper academic subject, accepted by universities and employers? Have we challenged them not to continue to identify R.E. with what they knew at school? Do we know them as people, so that they will feel sure 'you'll be all right with Miss B'?

2 *Form teachers' and options advisers' attitudes to R.E.* Have we educated our colleagues? Do they know the syllabus? It isn't sufficient to stick to the handbook summary, they need to be lobbied. Are they saying on the sly, 'You'll be doing general R.E. anyway, so choose something different for exams'? Are we investigating and challenging anti-R.E. comments from these members of staff which, if they do occur, can be so damaging?

3 *The child's loyalty to the teacher.* Without in any sense producing a hard sell, are we putting the R.E. case clearly to the children we teach, especially to two groups among them – those we know ·well because we've taught them or played football with them or whatever for several years, and those whom we know would do very well in the exam, if they chose it? Without in any sense abusing the relationships which we have established over several years, are we using them to the child's best interest?

4 *The impact of the Year 3 syllabus.* Since no pupil can have a real conception of what an exam subject will be like, much reliance in decision-making is inevitably placed on what the subject has been like, especially in the recent past. For this reason the 3rd Year syllabus and outside visits are crucial.

5 *The child's possible connection with a religious or church group.* Although modern R.E. seeks not to be confessional and the syllabus is in many departments not exclusively Christian, there are children who are drawn to an interest in R.E. because of outside religious activities. This can work against us: 'Our David won't be doing R.E. O Level, Mr

18

Copley, because he goes to church each Sunday and gets it there.' We can turn it to our advantage: 'You have a faith. You have an interest. Why not take an opportunity to study it, and other beliefs, further *and* get an academic O Level into the bargain?' Where you know the ministers, priests, rabbis, pastors, etc., you can discuss with them the advantages of your course.

By vigorously facing these factors as a department and by face-to-face chat with individuals in corridors, we can ensure that the numbers opting will begin to rise and will remain high. It is also worth discussing with your existing exam groups their reasons for choice and what influenced them. All this assumes, of course, that the syllabus for the exam provides interest and stimulus, and that the word doesn't get around that it's dull.

Some departments give pupils an unrestricted choice from six to ten A Level options offered by many boards. They believe this will motivate the students more and tempt more to opt. I can only give a very strong personal view, not substantiated by any research because none has been done, that this free choice is extremely unwise, for two reasons. First, no department now has the money to resource a new A Level syllabus chosen each autumn by each incoming Lower Sixth. Second, and much more important, I do not believe that there exist many teachers capable, with no more than a couple of months' warning, of teaching any A Level syllabus on offer up to the standard required for a grade A result. Any attempt to do this can engender serious lack of confidence among pupils, jeopardize results and in the long term destroy the option group. The only realistic approach is to decide in the department meeting what options staff are capable of teaching, what interests them most, and how this relates to book stock and allowance. Only then will it emerge whether a limited choice can be offered. I take the view that it is better to offer no choice, but to do really well the syllabus chosen by the department, than to offer an unequal choice to pupils not really able to grasp the full issues. At the same time, departments need to guard against using this maxim to prevent innovation in A Level syllabus choice.

The Sixth Form or Tertiary College presents special opportunities and problems for R.E. At its best, the R.E. department can offer a choice of syllabus because of larger student numbers; the options can be staffed by specialists who are capable of teaching them to grade A standard. O or AO courses can also be offered to students who missed

19

the chance or failed the exam in the Fifth form at school. The department can also play an adventurous role in General Studies courses.

Problems arise, however, because recruitment to courses is largely dependent on factors outside the department's control, such as the success of R.E. in the feeder schools. One college I knew, with a Lower Sixth of 250, had 30 students doing A Level R.E. but they were drawn exclusively from two of its feeder schools. Although on the surface 60 A Level candidates (when you add both Sixth Form years together) look like a very thriving concern in comparison to most school Sixth Forms, in fact from the point of view of R.E. they most certainly were not. Sixty out of some 900 A Level subject entries is, percentage-wise, much lower than that in many school Sixth Forms and the abandonment of R.E. at 16, if not earlier, by all pupils in eight feeder schools cannot be a sign of health.

It is also difficult for the Sixth Form or Tertiary College to influence the content and certainly the quality of R.E. in feeder schools. Pyramid meetings may produce agreement on course content and will certainly give the component schools and college a chance to exchange ideas and learn about one another, but at the end of the exercise the Sixth Form/Tertiary head of R.E. is dependent on others to do his recruiting for him. He needs to make staff who are interviewing in feeder schools aware of the problems if he is having a regular nil take-up from some schools. These teachers (assuming they are convinced of the value of R.E.) can then promote it in some schools as a possible third subject in an Arts or Social Science package for children who have not necessarily taken O Level. If even a handful can be tempted, word may begin to get around the feeder school to the next generation of Fifth Years that R.E. at the college is worth considering and is not to be ruled out because of their experience in school.

I am not taking sides in the debate on 'education at 16 to 19'; I am exploring the consequence of division at 16 from the point of view of R.E. More choice at A Level can be offered – at a cost of much less control over recruitment than in a school '11-to-18' or '13-to-18' situation. Those 60 out of 900 entries need to be at least 120 for health!

7 HOMEWORK IN R.E.

It is axiomatic to any experienced R.E. teacher that if homework is set in other subjects, it must also be set in R.E. But homework in any subject can in practice be presented as a sort of necessary torture.

'Now, let me see, it's homework tonight, isn't it? Now, what can I give you to do?'
Almost every teacher must say that at some time, if rarely. Regularly it should never happen; this brings the teacher's planning, attitude and hence ultimately the subject into disrepute.

In R.E. we need to see homework as an opportunity. After all, if we teach two periods per week, it extends the 'R.E. time' by fifty per cent. This means that the care which is given to lesson planning should also be given to homework. As a subject teacher I am conscious that I do not give this care and, although I am comforted by the feeling that neither do most R.E. teachers, I cannot justify bad practice. Here we have an opportunity to interest the child in making a (usually) drawn or written presentation – perhaps with a parent's hand in it too – that can extend or develop or test understanding of class work, or (less often, I suspect, than the theory books argue) develop the capacity to carry out a simple piece of library research.

A set of simple guide lines for homework is worth considering:

it should regularly lead to wall display;

it should more often than not give a child a choice of activity;

best examples should occasionally be seen and commended by the department head, as should any child who has made significant progress (see 'High R.Q. pupils', page 43);

the legitimate device of 'finishing off work from the lesson' should not be over-used, as it penalizes the more able pupil who has already done that and will just drift;

homework marks should be distinguishable from classwork in the mark book, so that work undertaken by parents can be spotted;

children who have failed to produce homework should be chased and set extra;

any library research which has been set needs to be checked in advance by the teacher – the department could perhaps produce a standardized list of possible topics and sources, with a visit to classes by the school librarian to help with study skills;

whatever work is set should be varied and so should choice, i.e., a child should not be allowed to opt out of written work into pictures for an entire half term;

over several years a department pool of homework topics on a given syllabus section, where they have gone well, could usefully be developed;

planning by the teacher is vital – experience teaches the teacher that where something sufficiently imaginative is set, many children will voluntarily spend hours on its completion.

8   USE OF VISITS AND VISITORS

Just as chalk and talk in R.E. has moved from the journeys of St Paul to better things, so visits should have progressed from trips to learn about the history and architecture of the local parish church, with their promotion of the church as an empty shell of mild antiquarian interest. A good programme of visits, once established, can be a way of doing useful and memorable R.E. which is highly cost–effective, because the pupils pay for the visits. An extensive scheme of visits can fulfil the following purposes:

1 it can bring alive in a first-hand way religious symbols, or a building used for worship, or the opportunity to meet a believer on his own ground;

2 it is ideally suited to a mixed-ability situation because children are able to absorb at different levels what they see;

3 the necessary letter of parental consent, collection of monies, etc. ensures that R.E. is talked about at home – this may enlist the interest of parents and help to revise their own conception of what we are about in R.E.;

4 in terms of pupil-teacher contact time, a visit can be the equivalent of several weeks of class-based lessons;

5 provided the visit is so structured as to avoid the 'goldfish bowl effect', it can give an opportunity to promote tolerance and get rid of stereotyping;

6 some disruption to the school timetable can get R.E. noticed in the staff room!

Over two years, the department in which I teach has been developing a programme of visits which involve all children each year in Years 1 to 4, with extra visits for exam groups. Each visit is in its own way integral to a unit of class-based work. Some visits within the local village are made within lesson time so that teaching time in other subjects is not infringed. The following summarizes the programme:

22

Year 1. Religion in the Village
This concentrates on externals and curiosities. It uses a quiz sheet, with two lessons spent on a walkabout. The whole is in the nature of a treasure hunt and includes graveyard curios, a site of Wodin worship, symbols outside churches, use of former church buildings, the significance of Church schools.

Year 2. Muslim Trail and Mosque Visit in Derby
This is a half-day 'package' set up in association with 'Education, Faith and Community', a Derby-based group helped by MSC funding, with the contacts, convenient siting and staff to help us to devise the course.

Year 3. Christian Studies Trail and Churches Visit in Belper
This embraces Roman Catholics, the Salvation Army, a 'high' Church of England church, Congregational and Baptist churches – another half day.

Year 4. (i) Village Churches
A visit within R.E. time to meet and interview believers and also to look at uses and problems of buildings.
   (ii) *Sikh Trail* and Gurdwara Visit, linked to a unit on Sikhism.
   (iii) *Visit to Salford* for exam groups, to follow in the Jewish and Chinese communities two half-day programmes from the Sacred Trinity Centre.

Year 6. Religious London for R.E. A Level (a visit we are still finalising): Westminster Cathedral; HQ of a national charity or a denominational HQ; Regent's Park Mosque; and a religious pop opera before the milk train.

Moving nearly 1,000 children in a school year appears a daunting task. There are few major problems, however, once the scheme is properly structured; this can be done by the use of pilot groups during the year before the venture is spread across a Year group. First, school and County journey regulations need to be checked. Then, to minimize disruption to other subjects, it is useful to plan the visit for a half-Year population, dispersing into form groups or sets on arrival.

The best and cheapest form of mass transit, in our experience, is by rail and we are fortunate to have a village station on the Matlock branch line. Party bookings can be at least fifty per cent cheaper than coach equivalents and the children prefer rail! For a long journey involving four forms or more, to charter a diesel multiple unit (162 seats) is

23

competitive with the price of several coaches. If no rail head is convenient, however, coaches or charter double-deck buses – used to shuttle several groups if it is a short-haul journey – will suffice.

Handling many children has helped us to devise a Code of Conduct for R.E. visits. This is read to each class before they go out. It covers behaviour in public places, in places in which we are guests, and safety factors such as platform-edge margins in stations which have Inter-City 125s running through at speed. The consequences of infringement are clearly set out and the Code forms a contract for good behaviour (see Appendix, page 77).

One of the spin-offs from all these visits has been an R.E. visit to a gurdwara one evening for parents. Their enthusiasm has inspired us to make a parental R.E. visit an annual event. Parents and children will remember aspects of the visits when lessons are forgotten. I believe, without tongue in cheek, that if visits are the core of Geography this is equally true in R.E.

It is easier, of course, to arrange a visitor than to arrange a visit. Visitors provide a stimulus that the resident teacher may perhaps feel he lacks – if, and it's a big 'if', the visitor can talk on a wavelength that interests the children, and doesn't patronise them. It follows that the department needs to build up a directory of name, phone number, area of expertise, availability, of those visitors it tries and finds successful.

In a big school the problem is always that your star visitor can't really be asked to speak to all eight forms in a particular Year group. That makes an unfair demand on his or her time, particularly since most schools will not be in a position to pay a fee and may have to struggle even to meet expenses. Occasionally a resident visitor, so to speak, can be useful; for instance, a member of a convent might be in school for a week and, in addition to formal contacts in lessons, could be 'around' to continue conversations and contacts in lunch hours and at break times; she would have longer to play herself into the situation of the school.

Despite the larger audience it provides, to put two classes together when a visitor comes can sometimes be helpful. This means that if the session should go dead, one teacher can escort the visitor for a cuppa while the other takes the class. Those readers who have seen a super 45 minutes degenerate during the last 15 or 20 minutes of a 60-minute double period, so that the final taste in the pupils' mouths was one of boredom, will readily appreciate the advantage of this arrangement. It also helps, if the pupils can cope, to make them responsible for the visitor (reception, showing out, thanking, etc.) though obviously many classes could not manage to do this. Where they can, with appropriate briefing, it may help the visitor to get on the right wavelength, and also make the group feel that this is their guest rather than the teacher's.

So much religious misunderstanding arises from stereotypes:

'All Roman Catholics believe that . . .'
'Hindus think that . . .'

The preparation for a visitor can be a good occasion to tackle this by examining, as the class prepare their questions, their expectations of the visit or visitor and by looking afterwards at the extent to which they were required – in the light of their actual experience – to revise them. It can also be useful for the teacher, during the questioning, to 'feed' to the visitor a stereotype of himself which the group may have revealed, without disclosing its source, and to invite a reaction.

Sometimes it pays to record an interview, so that the teacher, or other members of the department whose classes could not have that particular speaker, can use the edited highlights in a subsequent lesson. In an ideal situation the head of the department (or someone to whom he delegates) will have a collection of these tapes with an index of topics linked to their position on the track. The views of different visitors on, for example, euthanasia can then be selected for another class working on the topic at another time. The department in which I work used 26 visitors in two academic years. This should not be seen as a high total in a school of 1,100 plus.

Another ploy that could help as this team of visitors builds up is to hold a short social gathering – with some pupils present – by way of thanking them all, briefing them on how their contributions have fitted in and describing what future plans the department has in store (next year the Pope!). It could be very useful at such an occasion to appeal for information about 'unusual' experiences the visitors may have had of matters religious of which you may not be aware: perhaps someone has worked for two years in Lourdes, been a navy chaplain, lived in India, etc. These facts should be logged for future reference.

B The R.E. Staff

1 SELECTION

How far the head of R.E. will be involved in selecting new members of his department is, of course, variable and dependent on the will of the headteacher. I have known the scale of such involvement to range from heads of department who were told nothing until the appointment was made and perhaps only met the candidates in order to show them around the school, right through to other department heads who played as full a part as possible, from drafting the advertisement to being part of the interview panel and sharing in the final decision.

My ideal would be a team consisting of headteacher, head of department, R.E. Adviser and a representative of the governors working together to make such an appointment: this balances specialist R.E. and wider interests, two professionals inside the school with two people who have an 'outside' concern for the school's well-being, and it does not make too frightening a panel in terms of size. The significant interests are all represented.

The headteacher and the Adviser will, by the nature of the case, have far more experience in staff selection than the head of R.E. But he brings an intimate knowledge of the workings of that department which is not possessed by anyone else, and he should have a clear idea of the sort of person he is looking for. Selection is a two-sided process and the head of R.E. is vital to it.

First to consider is the range of general information about the school which the applicant will need. It is the headteacher's job to supply this, on the written specification and during the informal look round the school. Next there is information about the R.E. department in particular. The department head can give this in the written specification provided by the headteacher, and also on 'the day'.

Then come any other relevant factors – is the person appointed expected to help with assemblies, teach Chinese subsid., take over a third-form tutor group left vacant by the previous teacher, or run 'community service'? (This last is a wildly absurd requirement which schools seem to persist in inflicting on new staff since presumably no-one else wants to do it, though how new staff are supposed to have the community contacts is a mystery.) It is most important to applicants that department policy should be stated in summary:

'We see R.E. as an open-ended activity involving the study of different religions';
'Although we are committed to the study of religion, we do give detailed consideration to the Church tradition on which the school is founded', etc.

On interview day it is a help if the department head can provide not only a detailed syllabus, along with an indication as to how much of it is 'negotiable', i.e., being revised or open to revision, and a chance for candidates to inspect the resources, but also some representative samples of work done by children.

The head of R.E. needs to decide whether he wants to make any special comment about the information that will be gathered about candidates either from the form, by questions to referees or by questions in the interview itself. This still applies whether or not he will be present at the interview.

It is important not to ask candidates questions which require either text-book answers or answers of essay length to do them justice:

'Give your views on the last twenty years of R.E. curriculum development' would be much better replaced by something specific and short. Many of those reading this will have experienced as candidates (as I have), questions so laborious and ill-prepared that we have wondered in despair what on earth 'they' are on about, what we should say in reply, and whether 'they' could answer their own question.

There are several schools of thought about ways of reaching the final decision. Some use a grid system and award points, a method commended in the Open University's course E323 on senior school management. I worry that this purports to give an objectivity which is not in fact possible. At the other extreme is the gut response:

'I liked the look of her.'
'She does have the poorest references and nearly failed teaching practice.'

'Doesn't matter. I liked the way she looked me in the eye and gave a straight answer.'

I prefer a middle path, whereby as a team the panel first ask: 'Is there any candidate we can rule out?'

One or more names are proposed and, if there is total agreement, may be deleted immediately. Contested names need to be left in at this stage. Given that there are not likely to be more than four to six candidates at the interview, the group should now go through the strengths and weaknesses of each candidate in turn (unless one obvious star eliminates all the others from the outset). Where the decision is not clear-cut, it is desirable to avoid 'firming up' your own choice too soon. This is partly because you could be wrong and partly because, as head of department, you may find yourself landed with a successful candidate who was not your own first choice.

It is important that any panel of interviewers should remain open to each other's reasons rather than dig in and start firing flak at other positions. Nor can a head of department expect to dominate the choice against the feeling of the rest of the team. At the same time, if the decision is to inflict on you someone whom you seriously feel to be a wrong choice, you need to make that clear, with reasons. If the decision still goes against you, you need to give the appointee a fresh chance. We are *all* so different out of interviews! To continue to campaign against the choice would not merely be pointless and adverse to the department's health; it would actually provide the best possible argument for excluding department heads from selection processes involving interviews.

Selection should be followed up by meetings on several occasions, if geographically possible, before the appointee commences at the school. This provides not only a chance for much fuller briefing but also a more relaxed opportunity to get to know one another better and for the appointee to get to know other members of the department. Such a meeting is not simply a nice social occasion; it is very much in the interests of smooth and harmonious relations within the department.

2 DEPLOYMENT

Crucial to a department as appointments are, they are relatively rare. Deploying R.E. staff across the age range, on the other hand, is an annual activity and not often an easy one. At its extreme it poses the

28

problem: which classes do you give to an ineffective teacher? This process is more easily understood by using a case study than by a 'theoretical' explanation.

Let us assume a department of three R.E. staff with the following profiles:

Mrs A, the Head of Department, Scale 3, with a good Honours degree, eight years' teaching experience and a teaching commitment of 32/40 periods.

Mr B, a probationer R.E. teacher, with a good Honours degree and a reduced teaching programme in his first year of 30/40 periods.

Miss C, a qualified historian 'turned' R.E. teacher, with four years' teaching experience, some class control problems and a teaching programme of 26 R.E. and 10 History periods.

Mr D, a churchgoing Physicist deputy head, who will supply the necessary four periods required to balance the books (see below).

We will assume a six-form-entry comprehensive school with a small Sixth Form, which requires R.E. staffing as follows:

1st Year 6 × 2 periods
2nd Year 6 × 2 periods
3rd Year 6 × 2 periods
4th Year 6 × 2 periods + 4 periods of exam R.E.
5th Year 6 × 2 periods + 4 periods of exam R.E.
6th and 7th Years A Level 2 × 8 periods
General Studies 4 periods
plus 4 Community Service periods
Total: 68 periods in Years 1 to 5
24 periods in Years 6 and 7
92 periods in all.

The head of department is the person best placed to 'marry' staff to groups; in a school where he does not have this role he should certainly make representations to achieve it. As our imaginary Mrs A turns to her situation, she has four problems:

(i) what to do with the non-specialists?
(ii) what to do with the person whose control is weak?
(iii) what to do with the probationer?
(iv) how can she resolve any clashes caused by the fact that two of her staff are being blocked on the timetable by two other departments?

29

Where should she start? Before reading on, it might be an interesting exercise for heads of departments and aspiring heads of departments to get out a pencil and paper and block in the staff deposition as they would plan it, in order to compare it with my answer. Any vital information undisclosed in this simulation but which you would wish to know in 'real life' should also be noted. When you have finished your outline, read on!

My solution would be as follows:

I have already argued that the vital years in an R.E. department, especially a developing one, are Years 1, 3 and examination courses, so I would start my deployment as follows:

Year 1: 3 × 2 Mrs A, 3 × 2 Mr B

This is a break from common department practice, whereby often junior work is given to non-specialists. But why do we allow the vital first impressions to be given by the least qualified staff?

Year 3: 3 × 2 Mrs A, 3 × 2 Mr B

This is the vital recruitment year for exam options and so, again, is left to specialists. True, Mr B is a probationer, but he is working in each year in tandem with the department head and should have a ready source of advice to add to his enthusiasm.

Year 4: Exam course Mr B

Year 5: Exam course Mrs A (assuming she had started it with the group the year before).

Mr B whets his appetite with a prestige group, but with Mrs A a year ahead with advice and support.

Lower 6th: 4 Mrs A, 4 Mr B

It is desirable to have two teachers in each A Level year, while the department head has a foot in both camps! The other specialist(s) can slot around that and carry through groups in tandem with her.

The Upper Sixth is Mrs A's problem, assuming that the teacher whom Mr B replaced had been teaching them for some of their Lower Sixth time. Does she take all 8 periods herself, because Mr B has 'enough on his plate' as a probationer, despite his 10 free periods, or does she put Mr B on to it, adding a significant amount to his prepara-

30

tion and responsibility to a group in its exam year? I think that unless Mr B is brilliantly qualified in whatever option is being followed, he should be left out and for one year only Mrs A should break the rule of split Sixth Form teaching.

At this stage, of course, Mrs A has spent 28 periods of herself and 20 of Mr B. I suggest she 'finishes herself off' by adding 2 periods of 4th Year General R.E. and 2 of 5th Year, so that she can act as team leader to each group there. That completes her 32 periods. Mr B could be 'finished off' with one 2nd Form, 2 periods of General Studies, and two 4th Form classes of 2 periods, but left off 5th Year non-examination work in his first year.

In effect, of course, that leaves almost all the rest of the classes to Miss C. The rest in total are:

Five 2nd Forms of 2 periods
This would be a good move; it allows for easy preparation for the non-specialist, and junior work usually presents fewer discipline problems than senior work.

Two periods of General Studies
Not an unparalleled disaster, provided that Mrs A has resourced it well, because again there are few disciplinary problems.

Four periods of Community Service
This does not require standard classroom discipline, nor is it a specialist area, so – given with the right contacts and support – Miss C should survive.

The residue is the real problem:
Three 4th Year non-exam groups of 2 periods and 5 5th Year.
This looks so bad that it seems at this point as if the scheme may need re-writing. But all is not lost. Mrs A has one more card to play: the Heavy Mob! – Mr D, the deputy head, and his four periods. She needs to put Mr D into the two most difficult of the classes which remain for general R.E. in Years 4 and 5. He could kill Miss C's worst groups!

Like all department staffing allocations, this is a compromise. No final result will be perfect. Mrs A will obviously need to translate her fears for Miss C into support, though in the following year, of course, Mrs A will have two gains to look forward to; Mr B will be teaching an added 6 periods and he can be inducted into the 5th Form non-exam

31

R.E. so that he will – or should be able to – take some of the strain from Miss C. Mrs A will have to watch Mr D because if he does well she may want to fight with the head-teacher to keep him; otherwise a gain of 6 periods from Mr B may mean that the deputy head is switched to his main subject again.

In a department which you inherit, the pattern of allocation could be complicated in different ways and pencil and paper will always produce a different result. For instance: Mr/Mrs/Miss A as head of department – write in yourself, with your qualifications, experience and expertise; Mr B is 36 years old, a dedicated evangelical who sees the classroom as a mission field and was thwarted when you were appointed department head; Miss C is now a competent teacher with 10 years' experience but no formal qualifications in Theology or Religious Studies. Deploy that lot! One day you may have to . . .

Another principle involved in deployment, which has not been touched on, is that of continuity. In a big school, do you give priority to keeping the same teacher with the same group, if they are compatible, as the group moves up the school, or do you inject change as being desirable for classes and staff? And if you do opt for continuity where a relationship has developed well – I personally find it enormously rewarding as a teacher and a compensation for being a 'minority subject' in timetabled time – how far do you hold it as a priority over, for instance, the principle that each class should at some point be taught by a specialist?

If requests of this sort are made to timetablers, they need to know how highly you rank them alongside other requests you will have made – whether these are just castles in the air like your request for free periods on Friday 7 and 8, along with those from the other 99 staff, or whether you view them as in the three-line-whip category. It pays to put in these requests, however, even though the initial response will be Timetablers' Mystique Grade 1:

'Oh, of course, there are all sorts of constrictions operating on us that you wouldn't dream of',

because the timetablers *may* be able to meet them, at least in part. They may indeed discover, in something as complicated as a timetable, that – thanks to entirely different strategies within their chess game – they can give you exactly what you asked for. If they never know what your department would prefer, you are totally vulnerable to chance solutions.

Short-stay Scale 1 teachers are fairly common in R.E. in the sense that, despite the fact that there are fewer jobs in the education pond generally, it is possible for 'good' teachers to become department heads faster than in many other subjects, due to department size and to the significant number of non-specialists who are ineligible for such roles. A department of three or more may have in its most junior post a fairly regular turnover of probationer teachers, who move on after two or three years. There will be a County and a school policy for supporting these newcomers and, unless these policies are inadequate, they can be operated irrespective of subject taught. My concern is only to write specifically for the R.E. situation and so it can be briefly put.

All probationer teachers are very vulnerable: suddenly transformed from the artificial situation of teaching practice into 'full status', but without the experience to cope with difficult children or of teaching an almost full timetable over a sustained period of time. A final teaching-practice student may be teaching between 20 and 25 lessons out of 40 and can therefore prepare and polish them almost at leisure. In a probationary year some 30 or 32 periods will be taught for the full year, not just one term.

The teacher may, in addition, have the responsibility for a form and may be helping out with out-of-school activities. Almost certainly, in the secondary school, he will have some Fourth and Fifth year non-examination groups. They may be resentful of non-exam work, or R.E., or a new teacher, or all the lot! Here the probationer will need extra support in lesson planning so that there is sufficient variety to minimise the risk of boredom and sufficient quantity of material to prevent the probationer, to his great horror, from 'running out' in mid-lesson. He needs help in coping with awkward pupils because this is the sort of class where they are most likely to be a problem. This means having sufficient confidence in the head of department to be able to refer difficult pupils or to ask for help.

Another common failing of probationers is that in teaching they are apt to use difficult religious technical terms and so leave the pupils behind. Discreet examination of the exercise books used by the probationer's classes will show whether this is happening. It will then be possible constructively to draw this to the probationer's attention by comparing these books with some of your own.

The probationer also needs protecting from staff, not only to stop them from seizing on him to run rugby through the school by virtue of his having once played in his college's fourth XV as reserve, but also to ensure that unfair demands are not made on him to conduct assemblies because he is an R.E. teacher. At the same time he is more likely to be academically up-to-date than anyone else in the department – are these talents being used in the department, especially in exam courses? He also needs a chance to visit other R.E. departments. Perhaps the Adviser will arrange this as a matter of course. If not, the department head should take the initiative.

Probationers also need checking on the way in which they present religious ideas to children and the assumptions transmitted.

'God told Moses to lead the Hebrews' begs questions. How do we know? Why don't they talk about God in History lessons? What about the agnostic pupil?

'Moses believed that God told him' . . . begs fewer questions. An atheist can accept that. It is very important to get probationers to look at the assumptions they are making in the classroom about God and the sort of 'God talk' they are using. Is it what they intend? Is it what you intend? Is it educationally defensible?

Finally there is pastoral concern. Some young teachers find themselves in a personal dilemma over their own religious or non-religious position and the material they are called on to teach: for instance, questions of biblical interpretation, being fair to Sikhism if you are not a Sikh, dealing with Jehovah's Witnesses. Support is needed from experienced colleagues, perhaps more than the probationer realizes, and this in addition to the settling of problems common to all new teachers, e.g., class handling, with which the school and Authority should be helping.

4   STUDENT TEACHERS

One can only come to terms with student teachers by knowing their tutors well. This should be possible in R.E., where College/UDE departments are relatively small. Otherwise I am convinced that a latent suspicion exists: by the teacher, that the college tutor is a distant and impractical figure who would not survive five minutes in the 'real' world of the classroom and, by the tutor, that the teacher is peddling wares uncritically and looking for cheap labour from a student. The

34

worst teachers and the worst tutors may fit these stereotypes, but it is a pity to brand all the others.

As in the case of probationer teachers, some of the advice may come from the school's own system and may apply to students in any subject; some, again, is specific to R.E. From the school side, the head of department or his delegate needs to be able to give the student time to talk through problems, specifically problems of content and delivery. Even in a traditional topic like, say, the parables, the student may need help in interpreting the content in order to be fair to the theology; he may then need help in planning to teach them to, say, Second Years, in order to be fair to the children.

Where a school/UDE or college link is formed (and such links are to be encouraged) it is in the interest of all parties for the UDE/college to have copies of the syllabus, and these should be kept up-dated. The tutors themselves should from time to time visit the school and take lessons, with pupils of varying levels of age and ability. This does a good deal more than help the tutor to keep in touch; it has a very marked effect on his credibility with the students. A school/UDE link in R.E. might well be exploited through termly (or perhaps annual) seminars for staffs of both, and the seminars should include the UDE students. The agenda could be common topics in R.E.: teaching Sikhism; is neutrality possible?; the life of Jesus as a topic in lower school R.E.; Jewish symbols, etc.

Within the teaching practice supervision in R.E., special attention needs to be given to a number of points:

the student's use of religious language – was it pitched too high?

the student's implicit aims – were they confessional?

the student's ability to provoke questions on religion – and then deal with them; especially how the student deals with 'God talk' – what images does he transmit in his approach to this?

the student's dealing with religious authority – how did he use the Bible and other scriptures and what assumptions did he make about them? Were the children expected to accept these?

the overall image of religion transmitted by the student – is it of something alive, occasionally funny, often 'deep', or of something serious, flat and dull?

These issues need discussing with the student, who may not be aware that the impression he is creating is widely different from the aims he stated in his lesson notes. Speaking the truth is necessary here, but in love! Students are often anxious and may be victims of the common (and false) myth that R.E. is the hardest subject to teach. Taking them apart is of no value unless they can at the same time be built up. Yet feedback to the student, in a brief written summary from the department, is essential. It is wrong to expect the tutor to assess a situation which he knows so much less well than the R.E. teachers in that school whose classes his student is teaching. If the student knows the R.E. teachers already, through the joint seminar link, so much the better.

5   CLASHES AND COMPROMISE

Every situation in which human beings are thrown together in units of more than one will sometimes lead to tension and dispute. It is interesting that in most schools staff conversation in general is more frantic, more high-pitched and more liable to rows in the closing weeks of term, especially the long, long autumn term. Within departments, too, nerves can get worn and the department head, like the headteacher, has to learn when not to push his team too far, nor inflict on them another display, syllabus change or three-line-whip on a County course which will provoke resentment.

These occasions are temporary and very often linked to times of physical tiredness or of heavy 'seasonal' pressure of work such as exams-assessments-reports. There can be more fundamental and intractable clashes, sometimes of personality, sometimes specifically of an R.E. nature. The head of department, like the new headteacher, inherits a team he has not appointed and which he might well not have appointed, given a choice. Moreover, like the headteacher, he may very well be landed with them since, for all sorts of reasons, many teachers are disinclined to look for moves.

The two most fundamental causes of clash specific to R.E., however, are concerned with the philosophy of R.E. itself and with teaching method. The two actually relate to one another by way of their 'bridge', the syllabus, since aims will imply a particular content and that particular content will imply particular methods.

The most likely situation is this: a new department head (or probationer) moves in, committed to an open-ended R.E. involving at least some study outside the Christian faith. He finds a long-established member of the department – or, occasionally, head of department if the new arrival is a probationer – who has remained solidly in the past. He views change as anathema. Where do you start in this situation? I knew of one department where a dichotomy on these lines was so great that the head of department and his number two were teaching different syllabuses because agreement was not reached – so, amicably, they went their different ways, without resolving the conflict.

Granted the traditional, legally protected independence of the British teacher, it is difficult to bludgeon resistant teachers of R.E. into new ways. The department head, especially with the support of the head-teacher and R.E. adviser can, however, insist on syllabus, even if at the end of the line it is the Agreed Syllabus. The problem is that any syllabus can be taught in an unsympathetic manner, and whether the subject under study is biblical, Hindu, social or whatever, it can be undermined by insensitive teaching.

In other words, persuasion rather than coercion is the main source of change and that may mean that certain syllabus compromises have to be made. In any case the department head needs to know why the rebel is so awkward and stubborn. Is he at root frightened of change? Of learning new ways? Of a non-authoritarian approach to religion? That he can't cope with open-endedness? To get at these roots rather than write him off might start slow progress towards change. Equally important: what is his perception of you? Ask him?

If, however, there is still fundamental total opposition to R.E. which is defensible from recent research, Agreed Syllabuses, text books and courses, then a department member pledged to non-co-operation can be given a very rough ride. He can be required to defend his opposition to all this to the headteacher, and to defend his defiance of a new syllabus which has been introduced with the approval of the rest of the department and the Adviser and sanctioned by good modern practice; he can be compulsorily re-deployed within the school, at least in principle, by having his R.E. allocation reduced and by being moved into some other area. If his teaching is inefficient or incites parental complaints, then more can be done through the Authority.

The point I am making is *not* that the head of R.E. should be nasty to anyone unused to his ways or who questions the syllabus and mode of teaching precious to him, still less that he should ride roughshod over any opposition. In my travels as a college tutor I knew that it was a real (though very rare) phenomenon that a head of R.E. would be tearing his hair out about a colleague and would often feel quite impotent in attempting to cope with the situation. Most people will accept gradual changes if they are helped to cope with them – it is an unwise head of R.E. who forces the pace – but a tiny minority will not, 'not now, not never!' *You* may be working with one of them. If you are not, but are doing or about to do the round of interviews for head of R.E., gather as many clues as you can about your possible future team. You can always turn the job down, even if the system is mean enough to threaten to withhold your interview expenses should you do so!

In conclusion, be statesmanlike. Dialogue should be kept going for as long as possible. Change may have to be slower than you want if you are to take all your team with you. Consensus of the team is your most valuable lever against an individual rebel from the last century. Like any schoolteacher with a pupil you must avoid confrontation at any cost and certainly never provoke it *but*, if you sense that it is inevitable, you must make sure that with the help of the rest of your team, the headteacher and the Adviser, you are the one who wins.

6   ORGANISING YOUR OWN IN-SERVICE TRAINING

Many areas are adequately serviced in terms of in-service provision. There are perhaps DES Regional courses, Local Authority courses and even local working groups: the Christian Education Movement (CEM) or the Association for Religious Education (ARE), for instance. But other areas, particularly as regards provision for primary schools, may be a desert. Initiatives may have to come from individual schools, especially if there is no Adviser to help.

A planned day out at an R.E. Centre, even if the nearest large one is some distance away, can be an invaluable introduction to resources and a stimulus to schools to write new units for their syllabus. If the Director can be forewarned of the visit and the major areas of interest, he may be able to arrange staff help with the topics you have in mind. A subscription to the Christian Education Movement or the *British Journal of Religious Education* will also provide information about one-day or short residential courses in major centres. Their reviews of new teaching materials can also be a useful way for teachers in the desert to keep up to date.

If a consortium of local schools can get together they can perhaps meet the expenses of importing a known 'R.E. thinker' to lead a session, with subsequent group or workshop session to follow, so that a practical outcome results, linked to the classroom work of the group's members. More important, such a consortium can become a self-help group, developing new units based on contacts or materials within the local area. Once established, this sort of group often gains momentum. As in all self-initiated in-service work, it is the launching that is the hardest part.

C Routines

1 STOCK PURCHASE AND CONTROL

Most schools have a school-standardized or LEA-standardized system for this, so R.E. departments will have no freedom here. It is useful, however, to keep a departmental record of stock ordered, with date, and to own a department rubber stamp for use in various booklets which you may be given as links are developed with different local religious groups. A petty cash fund (cash from pupils who are paying to replace exercise books they have lost?) can be very useful for picking up odds and ends as members of the department travel or visit secondhand bookshops. Numbered textbooks for issue to pupils, so that lost copies can be charged, ought to be a department requirement even if it is not general throughout the school, and where copies are shared they should be numbered in the same way, in the names of the several people sharing them. The tedious job of stocktaking can have some of the ponderousness removed by involving reliable pupils. Stock shared with other schools (see D 7) needs careful monitoring and, if in the form of paperbacks, careful handling in transit.

Economy is sometimes false; one well-bound hardback set may be worth two paperbacks which, in hard use, may not survive more than two academic years. Where stock is used on a class basis, i.e. where one set of 35 copies does for a whole Year group, it is not likely to be lost as the books cannot be used for homework – another class may need them. On the other hand, books of this sort are particularly prone to graffiti and it then becomes very difficult to track down the authors. Spot checks, or books numbered in the back and given out in an order clear to the teacher, can prevent some of this or help in detection, though such activity still remains costly in terms of staff time. Graffiti-covered book pages, however, soon cause distractions in lessons and can bring the department into disrepute, giving its resources an air of tat.

Although videos and filmstrips are expensive to buy they may, when used in conjunction with your home-made booklets, be a very cheap resource; they can be seen/used by hundreds, even thousands of children without wearing out. Departments need to evaluate this in their planning. A school with an offset litho can also produce very professional-looking material at a modest cost – though watch the copyright laws!

2 PETTY CASH

This can be a useful asset enabling purchasing on the spot rather than by way of various forms, delays, the wrong stuff arriving, and so on. It could be funded partially by pupils as suggested above (C 1) and some schools will permit 'subs' from the department allowance in return for receipts. Parents travelling or working abroad can sometimes obtain postcards and artefacts cheaply and you should periodically appeal to them to do so. Engineers in Arab countries should be cultivated! I have obtained postcards, newspapers, prayer mats and Qurans in this way, often as gifts.

3 OUTSIDE SOURCES OF MONEY

Each department should examine any local charitable trusts, church finance or endowments the funds from which can be used for the purchase of, say, A Level books, even if certain conditions are applied: for instance, that they have to be available to members of the church making the grant. I was once in a department that picked up £100 in this way and it financed and resourced one A Level paper very well, leaving capitation for other uses. It is worth raising these questions with Councils of Churches or clergy fraternals, for where such funds do not exist these groups may be able to encourage donations and bequests which could provide one.

R.E. Advisers sometimes have money for R.E. curriculum development which can help, so do groups like the Council for Racial Equality. Grants of such monies will (reasonably) be tied to specific courses but again it gives room for manoeuvre with the precious capitation. Indeed it may be that, with the help of the R.E. Adviser, the local Churches, the CRE and others, the headteacher gives you ten talents and, lo, you have made ten talents more!

No one wants to proliferate paper work if it can be avoided, but a basic file should be kept to include the following:

1 copies of all syllabuses, updated annually
2 copies of past exam papers, internal and external
3 copies of all correspondence with outside speakers
4 copies of all stock orders
5 copies of all job specifications etc., relating to the department
6 copies of the timetables of those teaching R.E.
7 copies of all minuted department meetings
8 copies of all letters from parents specific to R.E. and replies
9 a list of any pupils withdrawn from R.E. and the reasons, if known
10 copies of all letters sent to parents about department trips, parents' visits, etc.
11 a copy of the Five Year Plan
12 copies of any general documents, e.g., booklets on exam R.E.
13 the list of 'High R.Q.' pupils and their progress (See C 6)
14 a list of addresses useful for pupils' project work
15 copies of all duplicated material produced by department staff.

5 PUPILS WITHDRAWN FROM R.E.

It pays to get the head's backing to try to engineer a personal meeting with the parents of any child proposing withdrawal from R.E., so that they can explain their fears and you can explain what R.E. is like in the school. All such attempts have to be based on the power of persuasion because, in the last analysis, the parents hold the cards on this. In my experience the most common cases of withdrawal involve the children of Jehovah's Witness parents and those of extreme atheists. One can compromise to some extent, but the tail must not wag the dog — one Jehovah's Witness permitted her daughter to remain in my lessons until I committed the 'doctrinal error' of teaching that Jesus was crucified on a cross; after that I was finished. The head of R.E. chose not to revise the course on this point, rightly in my view, rejecting the assertion that the statement was doctrinal and preferring to see it as very probable history! It pays to review withdrawal annually and to write to parents questioning whether they wish this to continue. Certainly if a school of

1,000 plus has more than six pupils withdrawn from R.E., the department needs to start asking why, and how this number can be whittled
down. No professional R.E. teacher would accept, I think, that withdrawal is any more than an anomaly in a subject whose existence has for
a long time been properly defended on sound educational grounds.
Departments also need to have a say in what happens to 'withdrawn'
children. It seems very unfair to other children to permit them to do
homework in another room and equally unfair to keep them in the
classroom in a non-participant way. It seems unreasonable for the
parents to expect extra tuition in some other subject. Each school has to
make its own decision here. R.E. needs to watch that withdrawal does
not become an attractive alternative, while at the same time the 1944
Act must be upheld. Another tight-rope to walk. . . .

6 MONITORING 'HIGH R.Q.' PUPILS

Some pupils stand out as naturals in R.E. A few of these will, of course,
be the high-flyers whose reports reveal that they are 'naturals' in every-
thing else as well. But for others this will be one of fewer subjects, or
perhaps the only subject, in which they excel. I nickname this 'high
R.Q.' – their understanding of religious concepts is high. These pupils
need our encouragement; they need to be known to the department
staff and their work praised by others apart from their immediate
teacher. They will gain in transfer from one teacher to another at the end
of an academic year, and we shall have given them a standard to keep up
in their new class. This is very good for their morale, especially if R.E. is
their only good subject.

It pays, however, to go further than this within the department; the
head of department should keep a private written list of these pupils and
should monitor their progress – the 'white book', perhaps! This group,
if properly encouraged, can become the nucleus of a future O Level
group and as early as the Second Year should be encouraged to think in
those terms. That is not to say that the list is unchanging or that pupils
not on it should not be encouraged towards exam R.E. Rather it is a
recognition of two things: that excellence deserves encouragement and
that there is nothing immoral in encouraging a pupil to see himself or
herself as a strong exam prospect. The pupil may still choose to opt
elsewhere, and certainly other departments will present more hard-sell
techniques than yours.

43

It is very important that the head of R.E. should know who are the able pupils in R.E. and that they should be periodically commended. In a big school this can be especially important. If the school awards prizes, there should certainly be one for R.E.; outside agencies, churches, charitable trusts, etc., may well help to endow one or more. If the school does not award prizes, the department could still organise voluntary holiday competition trails or puzzles, and award a small prize. At the same time it is equally important to recognize and commend effort as well as achievement, though this takes us beyond the 'high R.Q. pupil' discussion.

D Outsiders

1 PARENTS

From the point of view of the R.E. department, parents are much more than the biological producers of your clientèle. Their attitude can influence a child's progress in the subject and can be crucial when their offspring are considering whether to opt for or against examination courses. This is where the parents' evening and PTA contacts which you make with parents over several years can be of great value. I taught a girl in one school whose R.E. position in the form fell from 1/32 in her first two terms to hover around 23 to 27/32 for the next year. Her mother confided the reason, one parents' evening: Dad had told the girl roundly at Easter in her first year that the humanities subjects were a waste of time. I had to admit they didn't appear to have done him much good!

It follows that the R.E. department has two tasks in relation to parents: to inform and to liaise, as well as the task common to all departments, to report periodically on the child's progress. Very great care must be given to the wording of entries in options booklets.

General R.E., if described in such booklets, must be described briefly and in a non-exciting way, otherwise parents may take the view that if the child is doing some R.E. it is unnecessary to opt for more, i.e. the exam course.

As part of an information service the department might consider mounting an evening talk, with samples of children's work and of the sorts of resources used by teachers, including video excerpts and so on. This teach-in idea can have a ripple effect which spreads beyond those parents who actually turn up. Another ploy is to produce a booklet for parents about the school's R.E. courses, where options might lead and

45

into what sort of subject packages they might integrate. A Level R.E., for instance, can legitimately be stressed as a useful component of a history–literature group, or of a social science grouping, or a creative arts grouping, or as a subject with good training for would-be Law students in terms of reasoning, marshalling a case, etc.

Letters about school trips can contain background information too, rather than just a bald statement that 'your child's form is making a synagogue visit on . . .'. Better is a short paragraph: 'As part of a one-term course on Judaism and its symbols, your child's form will be making a synagogue visit on . . . The purpose of this visit is . . . and we hope your child will learn . . . Any information about Jews, Israel, etc., currently in the media would be very useful background and we ask that you help your child to "keep an eye open" for useful cuttings.'

Better still, initiate an annual R.E. visit for parents. Most of them are products of 'the old R.E.' and some will be keen to have some of the opportunities offered to their child, and to see some of the material used. Here is a possible format:

(i) Head's home/school general letter mentions R.E. visit and date, and refers parents to head of R.E. for detailed letter about proposed visit. They ask for one via their child.

(ii) Head of R.E.'s detailed letter sets out arrangements for transport, timing and contains a reply slip for those coming.

(iii) A week before the visit, an information sheet about the religious group to be visited is sent home to those parents going, via their child.

(iv) On the evening of the visit the group assembles at school, is briefed (briefly!) on the courtesies necessary on, say, entering a gurdwara, and perhaps shown a video or slide sequence on what they are soon to see in detail.

(v) the visit then takes place.

(vi) a week or so afterwards a letter is sent home to the parents who came, inviting comment and asking whether they feel a visit in the following academic year would be of interest and, if so, where to. I offered gurdwara, mosque, Hindu temple, synagogue, Religious Society of Friends (Quakers) and Roman Catholic church to parents in a County school, deriving the list from conversations which followed the first visit.

All this is not an elaborate device to seduce children into our courses. It helps us to teach children more effectively by knowing their parents better and it helps us by making the parents aware of the interesting and varied content of R.E. But no-one is objecting if it also strengthens our option groups . . . (Note: The question of dealing with parents of pupils withdrawn from R.E. has already been dealt with in Section C 5.)

2 THE HEADTEACHER

As far as R.E. (or, for that matter, any other subject) goes, the head is the power behind the throne. He may never teach in the department, but his support or lack of it can influence the department at every level – staff morale, scale posts, allowance for resources, willingness to permit school trips, placing of R.E. in option groups, number of periods per week. He makes the R.E. party go with a swing – or not! – and is probably as important as the head of R.E. to the well-being of R.E. in the school. So, while those outside secondary and middle-school teaching accept the image of the head as a remote figurehead, those of us who teach R.E. know that the head is far more central than that to the life of the department.

Heads of schools are as variable as heads of anything else, but because they carry the can they can easily become the person everyone likes to hate – a suffering-servant role, but with a better salary! Some heads assume the mantle of Elijah and decide to teach some R.E. as a way of getting to know the children. This can cause problems. When all the other R.E. teachers are doing Places of Worship, the head may be chatting about school meals with his First Year class. More rarely it has been the experience of former students of mine that the head has assumed a messianic status in regard to syllabus, and has intervened with all the confidence of a non-specialist to create confusion and chaos.

More common than any of these aberrations, in my experience, has been the head who has wanted no more than that good open-ended R.E. should thrive and should also include some M.E. in its programme. Such a head will take care in appointing the head of R.E., because he will expect professionally to delegate the running of R.E. without himself interfering any more or less than with any other department (unless something very unprofessional or incompetent is occurring). Increasingly headteachers have seen that R.E. is a specialist subject and that their role is to staff and support it.

It is the headteacher, therefore, who is the provider of manna – money and staff – and any head of R.E. who desires R.E. to succeed will

47

recognize the importance of good professional relations with the head if at all possible. This is not to suggest that the head of R.E. should be in some creeping 'yes–man' relationship, or that he should be a saboteur of other departments, but simply that the professional relationship should if possible be open and above board. That includes making to the head teacher any point about dissatisfaction with the deal of R.E. and not making it about him in the staffroom afterwards.

The head should be invited to department meetings and circulated with agenda and minutes whether or not he/she attends. If the R.E. visits programme is a suitably ambitious one, it is useful to take the headteacher on some of them. He or she can actually help, will learn about R.E. in the process and will not need as much 'staff cover' for absence as someone on full timetable! The Five Year Plan should not only be submitted to the head but also discussed at an early opportunity in order for the head to comment, especially on its realism in terms of budgetary requirements.

For the head of R.E. therefore, professionally speaking, the head-teacher is his best friend – though perhaps many heads of R.E. are appointed before they feel confident to deal with headteachers! The question still arises, however, how to cope with that tiny minority of heads unsympathetic to modern R.E. or convinced that they know more than R.E. professionals about what R.E. should be doing. It is too late to tell teachers under such régimes that hints of these attitudes must have come out in job specifications, or interviews, or informal chat with the outgoing staff they replaced. Nor do all R.E. teachers have the remedy of a former student of mine in this situation, who simply moved to another job. As a bachelor with no ties this was a luxury he could afford. If you are a man or woman with a partner at work, however, whose capital has perhaps been exhausted on costs involved in moving into the very job that has now become a trap, what can be done?

Full discussions with the Adviser should be an early help. He may help to influence the headteacher's dealings with the R.E. department. Consultation with a senior member of staff whom you can trust, and preferably trust to stand up to the head if necessary, can secure a good ally and a way of wooing the headteacher. In some situations it helps to be quite frank with the head and (seeing him by appointment, so that the conversation is less likely to interruption) to state 'When I was appointed, the job specification said . . . and my expectations were . . . You seem to be taking the line that . . . But have I misunderstood you?

What exactly is your position on . . .?' This might clear up genuine misconceptions on either side.

However desperate you are becoming, it is vital to keep channels of communication open, because you will either work in that school for some time or you will move; in either case you will need the head-teacher's co-operation. Consulting another member of staff is also vital. We are all human and it is just possible that it is the head of R.E., not the headteacher, who is mistaken.

It is always unwise to threaten a head (Adviser? Authority? parents? press?); not only is it professionally extremely questionable, but it is tactically highly dubious. The head holds most of the cards and unless he has taken some extraordinary step, like the abolition of thriving exam groups and the absorption of all non-exam R.E. into an integrated humanities course, against the express wishes of the department, parents and others – in other words effectively abolishing R.E. without consultation – such threats are counter-productive. Persuasion is the name of the game, and persuasion takes time, perhaps many years, and compromise. It may be that you should discuss with the Adviser the possibility of local moves, if you aren't a patient person.

All this is not to be construed as an attack on heads. In the main they are only too delighted to get good R.E. staff and to see the subject thrive. Nor can poor departments project the blame for their failings onto the head, except that perhaps he appointed them! But it would be less than the truth to deny that a tiny number of heads are – knowingly or not – choking R.E. in their schools. To this problem there are, as suggested, no slick remedies, but there are possible glimmers of light.

3   SCHOOL GOVERNORS

As far as most staff below deputies are concerned, the school governors may well be a rather remote body, with whom one has contact when staff are appointed and at formal school functions. The minutes of governors' meetings may circulate by way of the representative of the teaching staff. Since governors are charged with the general conduct of the school, they may well be involved with concerns that range from the state of the drains, through a recent suspension, to the headteacher's report on how the latest national survey on the teaching of maths is to be implemented across the school. Their involvement with R.E. may be nil.

In many schools this may well be mutually acceptable: the governors' remit is very wide; as R.E. professionals we do not often need their help with our concerns. There is little to be gained from producing reports and meetings to generate busy-ness simply in the name of liaison or goodwill. If, however, the governing body receives reports on the activities of various departments and their teaching programmes, R.E. should also be included or should ask to be included. Time to wave the Five Year Plan! Similarly if radical changes in syllabus are to be implemented, it is wise to consult the headteacher about whether the governors should be briefed; they can sometimes allay misplaced anxieties within the parent body or the local community. In a nutshell, therefore, the advice to heads of R.E. in County schools is: don't go to lengths to make extra work for yourself, but don't forget the governors either. In some circumstances they can be good friends to R.E.

In a Church school the situation may be very different. (For Church schools in general, see F 2.) There may be Foundation governors who are specially charged with responsibilities to the Church for the conduct of R.E. and school worship. One or more of them will be involved in appointing you! They will reasonably expect to know a lot more than their County counterparts about what is going on in order to discharge this part of their function. Since at least one of them may be ordained or a member of a religious community, they will have some specialist subject knowledge by way of background. This can be a two-edged sword! On the one hand they will have a concern, a sympathy and a background knowledge. On the other they may, very occasionally, misconstrue this as providing a professional expertise which equips them to tell you what you should be doing in R.E.

In such a situation it is useful to know the Foundation governors personally and to take the initiative in briefing them periodically rather than to wait to be questioned. They should occasionally be invited to visit the department. They can provide extra personnel to 'staff up' outside visits; in so doing they will meet children and see R.E. in action. They can be asked for useful contacts whom they may know for the bank of outside speakers on which you can draw. They should certainly know about the Five Year Plan, as they may be able to lean on the diocesan Inspector or Adviser to help with its funding.

Their statutory duty can in practice be discharged in such a way that they become assets to the R.E. department. Experience suggests that many 'Church governors' would welcome this use of their role. At the same time, as with headteachers, there may be a tiny minority who, 'let

50

into' R.E. departments, would actually be mischievous and unhelpful:

'I was amazed. The children were allowed to question basic doctrines. There was a course on Sikhism. Bibles were not always used. . . The bishop shall hear of this . . .'

Fortunately bishops are busy people! Nevertheless no-one wants to lose time in placating governors which should be spent on children and their education. A 'softly, softly' approach at first may well uncover potential problem people. Certainly if in this situation the head of R.E. has credibility as a worshipping active Christian, he is less vulnerable to this sort of attack. The headteacher or chairman of governors can often pull into line a governor whose interest and concern becomes interference in the professional conduct of a school.

Because it is in the nature of this book to try to anticipate problems, we again end on a pessimistic note. It must be repeated, however, that most governors will be delighted to help in the way that the R.E. department wants; and no department should ever feel threatened simply by being quizzed about its general policy. Accountability is not simply fashionable; it is also reasonable.

4 THE R.E. ADVISER

Subject to the very heavy case-load of Advisers, especially in relation to primary schools, R.E. departments should try to see as much of them as possible. Over a period of a year or two they should certainly be invited:

to a department meeting where major policy issues arise;

to spend a day watching lessons, looking at resources and teaching a class;

to spend time with the head of R.E. comparing cash allocation and timetable time to that given to other schools in the authority;

to lend support in conversation with the headteacher to new proposals for R.E.;

to consider 'covering' classes for the head of R.E. for a day while he goes off on a course or to an R.E. Resources Centre.

This is a counsel of perfection which few, if any, Advisers would have the time to fulfil in every point. Setting up courses, helping to appoint staff, caring for probationers, flying the R.E. flag in top policy meetings and travel at a national level will – rightly – swallow huge chunks of their time. The more an individual department can use an Adviser, however, the more it will benefit. The Adviser, too, will benefit by having more chalk-face contact with R.E. Perhaps the department can help him in turn by pressing the Authority for the appointment of a second Adviser or advisory teacher to share all the work which it has inflicted on him! This is a serious proposal. For too long we have seen R.E. as a 'survival' subject. Now we need the vision to see it as expanding, in school, at county level and nationally, and to press for this to happen. We must dare to ask for more, and more than gruel.

The R.E. Adviser's brains should also be picked on a number of key issues:

any new courses held by the Authority which he recommends you look at;

any new resources nationally which he recommends you to inspect;

whether he can inject any county money into your latest new syllabus;

your continuing theological education, subject content as distinct from pedagogy.

The Adviser, then, should be used; he is a major resource in himself.

5 OF UDEs AND CHEs

Despite the dissolution of the H.E. monasteries over the last ten years, a few bastions of R.E. still survive. These can be very important to school R.E. departments, even if up to twenty miles separates you. There are four areas, as a checklist, in which R.E. departments might be involved jointly with University Departments of Education and Colleges of Higher Education:

joint 'research' projects involving classroom testing and evaluation;

exchanges of one term between teaching staff;

loan of resources by UDEs and CHEs to schools, and loan of pupils' work to UDEs and CHEs;

schools taking students for teaching practice, block practice and visits.

If the local UDE or CHE is easily accessible for an evening, it could also be a useful development to encourage a joint staff seminar for R.E. teachers and the H.E. lecturers on topics of common interest. It seems realistic to think of this as a once per term exercise (See B 4). At present I am not aware of anywhere running such seminars, but they could be mutually useful and, while UDEs apparently continue to appoint lecturers on evidence of research ability rather than teaching ability, each 'side' could help the other. Such topics could include: preparing students for teaching practice; principles of assessment on practice; any joint school-based research venture; mixed ability teaching in theory and practice; teaching of a particular topic; religious language in the classroom.

6   R.E. CENTRES

Such Centres afford indispensable help by providing an opportunity to view resources, sometimes to borrow them, occasionally to make them, and also to meet staff informally in order to seek advice on hardware, software, and all the latest gimmicks, some of which are destined to become the standard resources of tomorrow. Where such a centre cannot easily be reached, it seems reasonable to second one of the R.E. department to it for one day each year to update the whole department on resources. If this were done by appointment with the Centre, its staff would know in advance what were the department's areas of interest, what time span to cover in referring the visitor to the loan or sample collections, and perhaps whether they could mount a roadshow of recent resources for a group of schools in your area. Directors of Resources Centres rightly feel that teachers can be over-concerned about resources at the expense of clear aims and syllabus, and that some teachers are expecting a package to be thrust into their hands which they can take into the nearest classroom and apply. For this reason, at least one Director refuses to demonstrate in group meetings without an accompanying lecture on aims and structuring of courses. Department meetings need to ask whether the fears of the Directors of some R.E. Resources Centres might be applied to themselves. Contacting these Centres is dealt with in E6.

Perhaps the most effective way of commenting on this is by a questionnaire:

a) Name all the heads of R.E. in schools of your type within a ten-mile radius of your own school.

b) How often have you met as a local group, formally or informally, in the last two years?

c) Can you summarize the syllabus in any neighbouring school apart from your own?

d) Have you purchased any resources jointly, to be used by different schools at different times of the year?

e) How many resources have you (i) loaned out (ii) borrowed, in the last year?

There is strength in numbers, particularly for the lone specialist. Time spent in devising courses can be reduced by exchanging units with other local schools.

E The Head of R.E. within the Total Curriculum

1 THE HEAD OF DEPARTMENT MEETING

Some schools operate a system whereby department heads are concerned only with internal running of their departments. Other schools
give them collective responsibility for the academic curriculum. In
others they assume 'pastoral' functions and are nominated as the first
buffer in the disciplinary line that leads eventually to the headteacher's
door. The heads of department meeting will reflect this role in the
overall school structure, so that the agenda may consist entirely of
relative trivia such as the dates for the internal exams, or whether
departments should provide file paper for Sixth Formers; on the other
hand, it may consider very fundamental issues such as whether mixed
ability groupings shall be used, or how options groupings shall be
determined.

It follows that, like other subjects, R.E. may have annually to bid for
survival at the option pools meeting; in other schools it may inherit a
secure unchanging pattern which can be an enormous help – or drawback, according to where you are in it. In the politics of one school R.E.
may be a threatened subject, fighting for survival in options along with
Latin and Music; in another it may have big groups, but be set against
second languages, so that the abler children will not choose R.E.; in a
third it may compete only with History, that godless version of
Theology!

In fighting for his subject, the head of R.E. is in a difficult moral
dilemma: as head of R.E. he must fight for it because no–one else can be
expected to champion the R.E. cause in the head of department
meeting. Moreover that is what he gets paid for! On the other hand as a
head of department, irrespective of subject, he has a responsibility to the
whole curriculum which can and should moderate his sectional and

partisan interests. Getting the balance right is vital and in my experience we heads of R.E. are such nice people that we tend to let the community take precedence over the individual department. This can be a form of professional suicide when our interests are crushed or dominated by the barons of English and Maths; perhaps heads of departments should read again the book of Daniel, and take heart!

Similarly, the whole department needs to anticipate what may happen to its proposals when these are mauled about in the HoD meeting. For example, to award R.E. two periods per week is palpably justifiable on sound educational grounds for which an impregnable case could be made. But the politics of the situation are more complex: for R.E. to gain a period, somebody else has to lose one – who? Although such a decision is ultimately the headteacher's, it may substantially strengthen the R.E. case if the department can propose a just solution. Someone, however, will almost certainly oppose it. Will the head of modern languages really permit his empire to be reduced by 5 to 4 periods per week. . . .? But he may propose it goes from 5 to 3 for the less able. . . . What does the headteacher propose for R.E. . . .?

The background to success in the department heads' meeting lies in two factors: not being isolated from all other departments – in other words you must canvass support for your proposals; and having good staffroom relationships, whereby the other department heads know what you are about in R.E. and do not simply resent you as the propagator of an obsolete subject.

2 INTEGRATION v CO-OPERATION

In some schools R.E. departments are offered the choice – be part of an integrated course in humanities or some other allied combination. In other schools R.E. is already part of such a course, but has the option to withdraw. At the risk of generating controversy and a vast corres-pondence from departments where integration is working well, I have to state quite plainly that I am opposed to integration. Having taught within such a system as well as outside it, I have reached the conclusion that in an integrated situation R.E. can very easily disintegrate and disappear, probably when the last specialist leaves the school. But first things first . . .

If an integrated course is offered to the R.E. department it brings some good possibilities:

greatly increased contact time per class;

a chance to influence the whole syllabus at planning level;

topics treated can be seen as a whole;

supposed pupil resistance to the label 'R.E.' does not arise;

in a team situation strengths are shared;

the R.E. specialist is not an isolated loner.

But look at the problems:

fewer classes will actually be taught by R.E. specialists;

the R.E. specialists may well be dissipated into aspects of the course which there are many other qualified staff to teach, so the school wastes rare staff;

the 'parish church' historical/architectural approach to R.E. tends to dominate the R.E. component of an integrated course in humanities;

treating topics 'as a whole' is as elusive a concept as the idea that 'a sentence is a complete thought in words' – it means nothing;

pupils are only resistant to the label 'R.E.' when they are being taught a certain sort of R.E., not all sorts;

integrated courses leading up to R.E. exam courses can actually increase the difficulties in recruiting for the latter, precisely because the pupil is not aware that he has done any R.E. before;

although the R.E. specialist is not an isolated loner, he may very well experience less job satisfaction because for most of the time he is not teaching his chosen specialism;

the politics of integration suggest that the Head of Humanities, or team leader, or whatever, is conditioned in his approach to integration by his own specialism, which is fine if he happens to be an R.E. teacher but not if he is drawn from another discipline;

integration can be used politically by schools to dispense with R.E. specialists and yet avoid breaking the law by dispensing with R.E., since components will still appear on the integrated course even though there are no R.E. teachers to teach them.

I am not arguing that every department should resist every offer of an integrated course in every circumstance. One area where it may work well is when an integrated course operates alongside separate subjects, for example in the Fourth Year, where non-exam R.E. may operate alongside a general studies 'life skills' course in which the R.E. teacher or department is asked to be one of a team contributing on the theme of 'Sexuality'. What is to be resisted is the approach taken by some schools that integration is automatically more beneficial than separation and that only the most fuddy-duddy, reactionary, ultra-conservative, bring-back-flogging type of teacher will be opposed to it.

Much more fundamental is the desire for inter-departmental co-operation, so that overlap in syllabus, which *is* sometimes helpful, can be planned and monitored rather than simply occur. Overlapping themes, for example when the historians do their inevitable 'life in a medieval monastery', can be used to good effect. In opposing or opting out of integration it is not enough to bury one's head in the sand, ignore the fact that the pupil is common to all departments and faculties, and teach as if he or she were just a piece of R.E. blotting paper – or any blotting paper, for that matter. Co-operation matters more than integration; many of the best integrated courses have arisen between teachers who know one another well and have worked together for years. What integration will never do is to rescue R.E.; it may achieve quite the reverse.

3   THE PARITY ISSUE

R.E. more than any other subject has inherited a Cinderella background which in some schools still persists. This is compounded at times by the Suffering Servant mentality of some R.E. teachers who have put up with the nonsense of, for instance, one period per week, making a few moans but raising no vigorous opposition. Much of what has been suggested here – the strength of department meetings, liaison with useful outsiders, a Five Year Plan – will provide ammunition to help tackle Cinderella situations. It is eminently justifiable on educational grounds to expect R.E. to have parity, but parity with what? Maths? I could argue such a case, starting with the premise that R.E. contains much more about life now and life skills and communication than Maths, but I have to be realistic and admit that the days when we shall be on five periods per pupil per week are not quite here.

It does seem reasonable, however, to argue for equal status with History and Geography, other 'human subjects'. Whatever they have in timetable time, options sets, capitation, staffing, should be at least equalled by R.E., because we have to service non-examination Fourth and Fifth Year courses as well. Once this principle has been fought for and accepted, the department needs to consider what steps need to be taken to implement parity and when these are best phased in. There is little point expending staff time in trying to work the unworkable – for example, to pretend that anything educationally useful can take place in one period per week. The challenge to anyone opposing that view is – do it in your own subject, or ours. The proper use of staff energy in such a situation is in the relentless quest for a fair deal in lobbying; in developing a good syllabus that you wish to introduce 'if only' – then 'when' – parity has been achieved; in canvassing support among the staff who matter; in bringing in the Adviser. The thrust of departmental push must be placed here until promises, timings, changes, have been agreed. Then, and only then, should we waste energy in trying to work an unworkable system. It's as simple as that, but the good nature of too many R.E. teachers has been abused and somehow the Cinderella situation lurches on in some schools.

4   PERSONAL AND SOCIAL EDUCATION

This is one of the new, great national bandwagons which is going to solve all the social problems in the present generation in school. Like many such bandwagons it provides opportunities and pitfalls, to mix the metaphor; as with many other bandwagons hailed as 'new, important breakthroughs', we find that in fact much useful P and SE went on in the past, even before the war, when dinosaurs roamed these islands! Our task is to look at this bandwagon from the point of view of R.E. (To look at it 'in itself', fully, would require a book in its own right.)

In some schools P and SE may be the only continuing form of R.E. at 14-plus. If for no other reason than that, we cannot afford not to take it seriously. Successes in units on such a course may provide the credibility within the school to re-establish a separate non-examination R.E. course again; there are hints from some HMIs that they would welcome such moves, provided the courses were worthwhile. Involvement in such a course, in the absence of non-exam R.E., may lead to the establishment of personal links which will encourage those pupils not following exam R.E. to consider it as an A Level. We may deeply feel that such P and SE courses are worthy in their own right; on that, as stated above, it is beyond the remit of this book to comment, though the very success of such a course could work against a unilateral move by any of the contributing departments.

There are some conceptual dangers to avoid if we are to involve ourselves in P and SE:

the problem approach, which somehow implies that life is a maze of problems – no solutions, no joys, no hope – abortion, wars, euthanasia, drugs, etc;

P and SE may imply that for older children and adults R.E. = M.E., that the 'God-talk', religious dimension is an option for children but not the real meat of life;

P and SE can be unbelievably woolly in conception and execution, and that is always a demoralizing situation for teacher and taught.

Similarly P and SE courses carry certain organisational dangers:

they often operate on 'short fat exposure' periods, sometimes known as the circus system, whereby a class is with a teacher for, say, four periods per week for a half term and then moves on to do another unit with someone else. This can create instability in classes and can over-expose the teacher. A heavy dose of a subject is not necessarily a more effective way to teach it;

the alternative, whereby each teacher teaches every section of the course, carries problems as to whether that teacher is really conversant with the material all the time and can sustain a two-year relationship, probably with a mixed ability class.

R.E. is *de facto* involved in personal and social education; it has to beware that, by being part of a social and personal umbrella, rather than an independent course, it is not contributing to an implied set of assumptions about the nature of R.E. and the (very small) role of religion in personal and social matters which it would do better to question keenly.

5   COMMUNITY SERVICE SCHEMES

In many schools these schemes are run by the R.E. department and seen as part of the concern of R.E. But should this be so? Is community service really analogous to practical/theoretical science lessons? How does community service differ from being kind in a quite secular way? In practice is it a way of getting the Fourth Year dossers off the school premises for an afternoon? Furthermore, do the projects really serve the community? Does the community want this sort of help? Are the children really motivated to provide it? Certainly visits to the indifferent by the indifferent or unwilling seems to be an effective waste of petrol and the school minibus.

Before taking on the onerous task of co-ordinating community service, therefore, departments of R.E. need to be satisfied on certain aspects of the exercise:

they need to be clear why this constitutes R.E. – if it does – and how it relates to the rest of the department's work:

they need to be clear precisely what they want the children to gain from it and to spell it out to them;

they need to train children for the tasks to which they will be assigned. It is not enough to turn them loose on an elderly lady for an afternoon and hope things will work out; it is the training which constitutes one educational benefit and which, interestingly, the children who are 'skiving' on this course will most resent;

children need to have some existing links with 'the community' and to have discussed in some detail what the community wants and what sort of placements will be possible. Letting bottom-set Fourth Years use the afternoon to visit their gran, whom they can visit any evening, weekend or holiday, is sloppy and undermining to the exercise.

I cannot see that community service in itself has any closer links with R.E. than school worship; in fact, probably, it has less. Nevertheless this statement is probably true of its relation to all other departments, except perhaps Social Studies. If the R.E. department considers taking it on, therefore, it must at all costs do a proper job, because one consequence of the woolly, muck-about image of community service held by some pupils is that R.E. will become tarred with the same brush.

The Head of R.E. has a crucial decision to make on this: can the needs of the course, the community and the pupils involved, justify his appointing himself or one of his team to be responsible for setting up the contacts, organising the visits, training the youngsters and doing follow-up work? Can all this justify further removal of what is probably a small department's team from work on R.E. course development and the many other links and tasks suggested in this book? Or, candidly, should he insist that community service be run by one of the major departments that is better staffed to do it? Community service schemes can work very well, but the first condition for success is major staff input.

6   THE PRIMARY SCHOOL

As far as R.E. goes, the primary school is simultaneously more simple and more complicated than the secondary sector. More simple, because in an environment which is basically a one-teacher, one-class situation, the 'GP' teacher who will be guiding the class through most of the curriculum will not have the problems of getting to know the children, neither will the primary teacher have the constrictions of external examination courses. More complicated, because there may well be no R.E.-trained specialist in the school at all, especially in the small primary school. Whoever is designated as R.E. co-ordinator is therefore not very likely to be given time to plan courses, nor an up-pointing in salary; the whole of his R.E. training, moreover, may have been restricted to a short general course of one hour a week for a few weeks as part of the general education components in a primary B.Ed. degree or post-graduate Certificate course. However well trained he was or was not, this teacher will not be able to give undivided attention to R.E. because of the other necessary demands on his 'general practitioner' status which require him to keep abreast of developments in the teaching of reading, maths, science, etc. Nor is it likely, because of the very large number of primary schools in most LEAs, that the R.E. Adviser will be able to visit the school personally.

Bearing in mind the many demands made on the primary teacher, whatever is proposed as a method for co-ordinating R.E. in the primary school must be realistic in its demands on time. It is in the primary sector, however, that the Agreed Syllabus can come into its own. With the non-specialist co-ordinator of R.E. particularly in view, I suggest the following process as both realistic in terms of available teacher time and appropriate to the situation.

First, study the County Agreed Syllabus, checking that it has been produced (or at least revised) in the last ten years. Read the secondary section as well, so that primary R.E. is seen as part of a continuing process from 5 to 16. At this point it can be very useful – indispensable if your own Agreed syllabus is dated – to compare those of neighbouring authorities or any others recently produced as a possible source of more ideas about units and resources. CEM membership also brings with it a primary mailing, reviews of resources and details of courses. Many LEAs will mount a primary R.E. course if asked and some do so regularly on an annual or biennial basis. In a Church school the diocesan Adviser should certainly be consulted. All these may spark off more ideas for schemes of work.

After this 'gathering' process, the R.E. co-ordinator should be in a position to draft a scheme of work with the needs of those children in that particular school in mind. It is useful at this point to liaise with the secondary school into which the pupils will transfer. What both schools do is interdependent and while children can and should tackle some topics, 'Christmas', for instance, differently at different ages, heavy and too obvious overlap is better avoided. It may be convenient to use a pyramid meeting annually, whereby several primary schools liaise with the secondary school over syllabus at the same time; this does imply, however, that the primary schools will be covering roughly the same material. Another reason for a pyramid link is that the secondary school may not in fact be using the Agreed syllabus. Sometimes the fear that they may not touch on topic Q in the upper school can lead primary teachers into tackling topics that are really too advanced for the con-ceptual development of their own children. Better to hammer out topic Q at a pyramid meeting, to see who should do it and when.

Once there has been consultation with the secondary sector and possibly with other neighbouring primaries, the R.E. co-ordinator is much nearer to finalising a programme for the school. He/she will by now have arrived at a set of aims and objectives and probably a list of themes or topics. This is where the teacher's expertise within his own school comes into play. The aims and topics can be apportioned to different age groups and times of year, discussed with the rest of the staff and related to other known topic-based work such as History. It may be that when, at the end of this exercise, a syllabus emerges, it will be – although geared to flexible modern primary methods – still none other than the Agreed syllabus with a few changes. This does not mean that all the research and consultation has been wasted. That should still have 'sharpened' the Agreed syllabus and turned it into what it could never have become without such consultation – the relevant syllabus for *your* school.

The finalised course must then be resourced. Recent Agreed sylla-buses have been very helpful in recommending resources. Further help can come from Church and County Advisers, R.E. Centres and, as with so much primary school material, some can be homemade.

63

Having produced resources or obtained them elsewhere and set the course in motion, the co-ordinator's next job is to monitor the course as it proceeds. Much here depends on the nature and size of the school. One meeting per term seems not unreasonable for R.E. in a 'GP' situation, but it may be possible to transact R.E. business in the informal atmosphere of the staffroom in the lunch-hour and dispense with formal meetings altogether.

Tactful handling of staff is vital. They may resent being co-ordinated at all. Mrs Z may have done the Joseph story for years because it leads to colourful display work, but she may, in so doing, have omitted any religious mileage at all. Telling her to stop using that story is unlikely to be conducive to good relations. Injecting a dimension of R.E. might be. There is a tendency in some primary R.E. to secularize religious (especially Old Testament) narratives in order to make them 'easier' for young children. The R.E. co-ordinator needs to call attention to the danger of doing this, namely that secularizing the stories, 'missing out the God bits', removes the religious element – they may still be good stories, but they have ceased to be R.E.

In Church primaries, the teacher responsible for R.E. needs to consider with care how the church link might be used and related to R.E. There are three components in this for the child:

the church building, which can be used well for a study of Christian symbolism and badly, for R.E., for a historical survey;

church personnel, especially but not exclusively the vicar or priest, who may be known in school as chairman of the governors and to the child as conductor of school worship;

church worship on occasions when the school as a body might be in church: harvest, school Eucharists, etc.

The educational possibilities in the components need to be developed and written into the R.E. scheme of work at appropriate points.

For the teacher who has been pushed into co-ordinating R.E. against his will and with no real subject knowledge there are no slick solutions. He cannot pretend an expertise which he does not have. He may, however, gain more insights into primary R.E., aims, contents, methods, which takes us beyond the brief of this book, by use of the following:

What can I do in R.E. by Michael Grimmitt (Mayhew-McCrimmon).

First School R.E. by Terence and Gill Copley (SCM Press).

The Religious Education Directory, which covers England and Wales, edited by Brian E Gates, is a mine of information for primary, middle and secondary teachers. It lists LEA and diocesan R.E. Advisers, resources centres (with opening hours), contact addresses and phone numbers. It also dates the agreed syllabuses, and lists journals for R.E. and for R.E. in HE, along with much other useful information. This Directory is available from the R.E. Enquiry Service, St Martin's College, Lancaster, LA1 3JD.

Together is a magazine published by the General Synod Board of Education (9 issues per year) in which primary Church school and Sunday school teachers can share practical ideas (plays, services, stories, etc.) they have devised themselves. Subscription details from the Circulation Manager, *Together*, Church House, London SW1P 3NZ.

F   Aspects of the Head of R.E. Image

1 SCHOOL WORSHIP

In a County school it is interesting to note how many staff still expect the R.E. staff to possess some mysterious expertise which enables them to conduct school worship. Perhaps this is the last residue of the vicar-figure image of the R.E. teacher. It is certainly still expected in many schools that the department will organise the assemblies. It is possible to be endlessly pessimistic on this subject and an entire book could be written on what we might do with school worship, though some would claim to answer this question more succinctly!

Basically, now that the model of the mini-church or unde-nominational service has collapsed, there is a national search for a model to justify our practice. There is no reason why the R.E. department should not convene a staff discussion to air the whole matter and establish a suitable model for their own school. Indeed, a school could use several models simultaneously; there is still value in defining them rather than just drifting along in uncertainty. Lack of confidence about school worship has become an epidemic. All those in the County school know what they should not be doing; they are less certain what they should be doing.

It is possible to use assemblies in various ways:

for worship and business matters – these meetings work much better if kept separate;

worship can be used to evoke a sense of wonder or to look at an issue as a whole, not split into separate compartments;

worship can be developed in a 'Thought for the Day' mould – 'here is something I care about that I want you to consider . . .';

worship can occasionally be a focal point for R.E. teaching despite the mass audience, e.g., in a white 'Christian' school, a visit by Divali dancers as the climax to a course on Festivals that concluded with Divali;

worship can be developed over several years with children as a short, silent meditation using music, words, pictures, dance, to set a train of thought in motion;

worship can be used to express some common value of the school community, though this should be expressed as something much higher than the anti-litter homily by a senior member of staff;

worship could be developed as a vehicle to express the concerns, fears and hopes of children themselves, in which case a staff-pupil group to plan and think through the issues would be essential.

On each of these ideas, and others, a chapter could be written. Our concern is a narrower one – how far should the R.E. department be involved?

I suggest we should work towards the following situation: if required to organise school worship, we accept that as a temporary situation and do it! During the first year we should be bringing about a number of changes:

initiating a thorough staff discussion in which we provide the positive input on what can be done, perhaps developing some of the above models;

involving a wider team of staff and pupils in the conduct of worship;

tactfully and professionally sharing some of the ideas with youngsters – 'these are the boundaries, these are the possibilities' etc;

developing, with some commercial help, a resource bank of assembly themes and material – using school funds, not the R.E. allowance.

In other words, we should be promoting the idea that school worship is no longer the responsibility of R.E. but of all staff; we are prepared to share this, but the traditional image of worship can be replaced by alternatives that gain the assent of staff and pupils. A variety of models, a variety of people responsible, a variety of techniques and format are all needed. There should be separation of the business assembly with its necessary notices, sports results, admonitions and commendations. R.E. should therefore make the transition from the beast of burden which carries the full weight of acts of worship, to the enabler, working to release the talents in staff and pupils, inspiring the confidence to present their concerns and affirmations so that, in our particular school community, some common values and a way of expressing them will begin to emerge. Such acts of worship may not much resemble the old hymn-reading-prayer, but they may be more real *as worship* to those people in that situation.

2   THE CHURCH SCHOOL

Church schools offer some advantages to R.E. departments, provided that the department is able to establish that R.E. is an independent subject like any other, not an arm of the Church functioning within the timetable to produce pew-fodder. Within a Church school, R.E. ought to be able to make certain assumptions, and should be vociferous if they are not accepted: parity issues should never arise here, nor should any question of an under-financed department; the Church school should give the strongest support to R.E. – positive discrimination – not because R.E. = Sunday School or Junior Church, but because the Church has a vested interest in truth and in people being informed about religious matters in order that whatever conclusions they reach as adults about religion may be based not on misconception or infantile under-standing but on mature knowledge. It follows, therefore, that open-ended R.E. may reasonably be expected to be compulsory up to and including exam level in a Church school. The department can then exploit the fact that all children are following the course by offering a choice of syllabus, and can teach two or more syllabuses to different groups, letting the option for syllabus determine group setting in the first instance.

It seems reasonable also, as part of education about the community in whose tradition the school stands, that R.E. should undertake some special and detailed treatment of the Church or religious body which originally provided the school. Again, there is no reason why this cannot be done in an open-ended way, though if it is to be educational it can only be seen in the context of other groups, i.e., ecumenically, because person C can only truly see himself as an Anglican in relation to Anglican tradition and history, to his personal upbringing and to person Y as a Roman Catholic and person Z as a Quaker. I would want to add 'in relation to other religions as well', though this in no way presupposes that each must be taught in equal length or depth.

Similarly in a Church school R.E. can be reasonably expected to deal in some detail, but again openly, with Christian worship and with Christian festivals. In other words, being in a Church school has a very definite effect on syllabus, but not on the professional approach to the teaching of a proper academic subject.

It is vital to discover, before accepting an appointment in a Church school, whether the establishment there expects R.E. to be concerned with religious education, Christian education or Christian nurture. If particularly the latter (which may be held to be a proper concern of a Church school) then it is necessary to discover whether R.E. is expected to undertake this, or whether it comes by way of catechetics or the school chaplain or the total school environment. Whatever the case, you need to feel sure you can go along with the establishment or make changes if its expectation of R.E. conflicts either with itself or with your own.

Ordained staff or members of religious orders need to resolve not only the conflict between their religious profession and their concern as educators in religion; they also need to resolve this conflict in the eyes of their pupils. It will be hard for children to perceive any adult in two distinct roles, but older children may learn by talking it over with them.

Links with the diocese may help; it is useful to explore, through contact with the Diocesan Director of Education or the Schools Adviser, what is diocesan education policy.

Perhaps the R.E. teacher is more vulnerable in the Church school than in the County school to pressure from outsiders. The head may keep a special eye on R.E.; so may the Foundation governors, the diocesan inspector, parents with an axe to grind, local churches and clergy. If the head of R.E.'s role is further complicated by ordination, he will be further susceptible to Church discipline. Is sound doctrine being taught? Are children reading the Bible? Aren't they spending too much time on Islam? Shouldn't R.E. be linked to the confirmation course? All these and similar questions could explode in the face of the head of R.E., who needs to be sure that the department can withstand an occasional buffeting and that the headteacher is prepared to defend its position.

The Church school, then, is to R.E. another opportunity. It can offer contact at first-hand with a living religious tradition which takes religious studies seriously. If things go wrong, however, a collision of aims may ensue between those concerned with education and those concerned with propagation: it is arguable that in a Church school both

69

have a place, but the dividing line must be clearly drawn and heads of R.E. need to know before they are appointed on which side they are expected to stand.

3   OF CUs AND HOLY CLUBS

Many County schools have within them Christian Union or other Christian pressure groups which meet for worship, or discussion, or other involvement with specifically Christian concerns. The R.E. department may very well contain some Christian staff. Here the role-blurring appears again. Should they be willing, as individuals, to run such groups? Does the teacher turn preacher on Mondays at 12.30? My view is that it is better both for the R.E. department and for the CU or club if the latter is run from the staff side by a teacher other than an R.E. specialist. This is better for the R.E. image, as it avoids confusion, and also better for the Christian image, reminding children as it does that Physics and History teachers are quite as capable of Christian living and leadership as academic R.E. specialists. Some CUs may experience mild conflict with modern R.E.: 'they' (its teachers) ought to be more Christian, to read the Bible more in class, to be willing to take a more openly Christian position, etc. Useful discussion can arise from comments of this kind.

It might be possible to start a more broadly-based R.E. club, not limited to the Christian tradition nor 'pushing' a religious view but giving more chance for discussion and for making regular visits to acts of religious worship as opposed to visiting empty buildings, the shells of worship. As an optional activity this could greatly enhance the R.E. of the pupils involved. Such a club or society could greatly facilitate staff-student contact, the cause of R.E. and the personal religious search of many pupils by whom a conventional religious society would be seen as narrow or 'not for me'. Such a club could therefore supplement, and need not rival, a CU or specifically devotionally-geared group. It could undertake visits to different groups at worship, both from the wide range of Christian options and from other faiths, and invite their leaders into school.

4   LIVING IN THE CATCHMENT

Whatever one's subject, there are pros and cons to living in the catchment. At the worst it may bring a brick through your window; at the best, a 'normal' out-of-school relationship with pupils and their parents, and a chance to learn about them outside school. It can bring anxious or irate parents onto your doorstep, anonymous telephone calls, pleasant chats in the street or the Co-op, and an opportunity to talk in a relaxed way about 'non-shop' things. All this applies whatever one's subject. But are there factors special to R.E.? There is one which is crucial.

The 'cover' of the R.E. teacher, i.e. his own religious position, will be blown by living in the catchment. It will almost certainly become known to his pupils whether he attends a place of worship or not and, if he does, which one. This is not in itself bad – no teacher can nor would desire to operate as a total enigma – but on the other hand it can lend to labelling in the pupil's mind:

'I'm an agnostic. How can I talk to X, who's a pillar of the Pentecostal church?'

'As a Roman Catholic how can Y help me, a Baptist?'

'My Dad says the Methodists are against drink and Z is a Methodist.'

Similarly a church-going R.E. teacher may have to fight expectations made by his church. 'Of course we desperately need you as a teacher to run the senior Sunday School group' – and teach some of your young-sters in a totally different way on Sunday. Spare them that!

At the same time the dangers of this sort of identification can be overcome to some extent by an ecumenical involvement, and by talk-ing to children who say 'I saw you at Mass last Sunday' about the dangers of labelling, and the difference between personal commitment and commitment to religious study and academic enquiry. Although the decision to live in the catchment or not does carry implications for R.E., these implications should not therefore be decisive in making the choice; invariably the factors already listed and others – house prices, the school to which your own children may go – will be much higher on the list.

5   AS A VISITOR TO IN-CATCHMENT WORSHIP

Whatever the religious beliefs and disbeliefs of the teacher and wherever he is living, there are considerable advantages in periodically attending worship at churches, synagogues, etc., within the catchment. These advantages are principally:

to gain first-hand experience of what is 'on offer' in that area;

to meet some pupils on their own religious ground;

to become known to churches whose premises and personnel the department may be requesting to use;

to extend the teacher's own experience of religion;

to collect magazines, documents, etc., for use in school;

to view interiors of buildings normally locked, for possible future use.

Of course a teacher who is a practising member of that particular faith will gain a personal benefit by worship with them. It has to be said that R.E. teachers have not always experienced a range of worship at first hand, and that, curiously, religious commitment is a disincentive to do this because if you worship within a tradition you enjoy, at a local place of worship in which you have perhaps become an office-bearer, it is hard to take a day off to go on tour!

G   Next Step?

Many teachers will find that, because of the shortage of good, specialist R.E. teachers, they achieve head of department status more quickly than is usual in some other subjects. After a time (nowadays one would suggest not less than five years) such teachers will want to consider their future, even if this final decision is to stay put for longer, or for the rest of their career. The problem, of course, as in other subjects, is that the higher you rise, the less subject teaching you do; perhaps heads of department should pause and reflect that, however dissatisfied they are with their lot, the head of department in a school has one of the most creative jobs. He isn't an administrator, simply oiling the machine so that others can teach efficiently, nor is he the axe man who bashes the disruptive, nor even the counsellor whose frustration is the tension between seeing one pupil now and knowing that he should be teaching a class.

The head of R.E. can be highly influential, even in a democratic department, in choosing syllabus, resources, deploying staff, timing units: in short, for directing the education of perhaps hundreds, even thousands, of pupils in a vital subject.

It may be that head-of-house or head-of-year type of work is the most appealing next step, but before it is taken you may have to surrender much of your autonomy until eventually, as a headteacher remarked to me, your teaching becomes residual, not central.

Vacancies for lecturers in CHEs and UDEs are few and usually require research experience. Here careful thought has to be given to whether you care to carry on in full-time R.E. without the children. The same applies to advisory posts where employers, in any case, are beginning to look for experience in school at a higher level than head of department.

Certainly all teachers will at some time reach the point where, from

73

choice or circumstance, they stop. It helps if this point has been reached from choice and is not regretted afterwards because it eventually proves either too low or too high to be satisfying. My own view is that R.E. is an excellent and fulfilling area of work, both in itself and as a bridge to something else which may eventually take precedence in your own career priorities. To teach it, to have taught it, is not to have taught what some describe as 'the most difficult' subject, but the most challenging and ultimately – in my view – the most rewarding subject of all.

Appendix 1

Dear Parents,

Thank you for your interest in this visit expressed through your child. We have pleasure in sending you details.

With the help of various external agencies our pupils visit the Muslim community (Year 2), the Christian groups in Belper (Year 3), the Sikh community (Year 4) and, for exam groups, the Jewish and Chinese communities in Salford. It is through these contacts that this visit has been arranged.

Rather than simply arriving at the Temple and being shown round with little or no prior knowledge of Sikhism, we thought it might be helpful to parents who come on the visit to have the opportunity to do a little background preparation as follows:

parents coming will be supplied in advance with a 'Sikh Information Sheet';

on 10th November we will meet in school at 7 p.m., to show a 15-minute video on Sikhism and to describe very briefly the proper customs to observe on entering the Temple;

we shall then leave for the Temple at 7.30 approx.;

the visit will conclude at approx. 9 p.m., with customary hospitality at the Temple.

Please note that men and women will require suitable head covering to wear inside the Temple (scarves for women are acceptable).

We hope that you will want to join this visit – and if any slight nerves about 'what to do, when' concern you, do come to the short 'teach in' first!

Yours sincerely,

SECOND YEAR R.E. MUSLIM VISIT

Dear Parents,

As part of classwork in R.E. this term your child has been studying Islam with the help of books and films. But the climax of this work is a visit to Derby Muslim Community, including an urban trail and mosque visit.

This will take place on the morning of 15th March (2R, C, F) and 17th March (2H, W, A). We shall travel by rail from Duffield, returning in time for lunch.

The cost will be £1.45. This includes return rail fare to Derby and a folder which the child will keep, containing various booklets on Islam produced by the Muslim Information Service, Arabic Calligraphy, and the urban trail booklet. In the case of children of B.R. employees the charge is £1 and they will have to pay the rail fare on the train, using their Privilege Tickets.

Please return the enclosed slip and if payment constitutes a difficulty do not hesitate to contact me.

Yours sincerely,

HALF DAY VISIT TO INNER CITY DERBY

Dear Parents,

The R.E. Department, in association with Derby Cathedral Man-power Services Project and the Derby Council for Racial Equality, is planning a new teaching scheme subsequently aimed at the whole of the Fourth Year in this and other schools in the area. Your child's form has been selected as the trial group for the new scheme, which will involve a half-day visit to Derby, partly in R.E. lesson time. The day planned is Wednesday 10th March.

The visit will include a guided walk, a chance to meet youngsters in a multi-racial school, a visit to a community centre and to the Sikh gurdwara (Temple). The aim is to enable youngsters to see something of problems and opportunities in the inner city and to see the culture and religion of some immigrants.

The cost of the visit will be 75p (approx) to cover coach transport and your child may want to bring money for morning refreshments provided by our host school. We shall be back for lunch.

I hope you will strongly support this visit, both as worthwhile in itself and to enable us to plan something for many more of our young people.

Yours sincerely,

Each teacher should go through this with his form before every visit:

1 Pupils must walk sensibly on pavements and not obstruct members of the public.

2 No-one must lean out of windows on coaches or trains.

3 Chewing is not permitted on 'walk-arounds' or inside buildings in which we are visitors.

4 On stations, pupils and their baggage must be at least two feet clear of the platform edge. Because of the suction effect of passing fast trains, bags should not be left unattended on platforms.

5 Trains and coaches should not be boarded until staff give permission.

6 As guests in places of worship we should show respect. In gurdwaras and mosques this is especially important.

7 Once this Code has been given to a class, punishments to those breaking it will be given without further warning.

Appendix 2

Preamble:
Definitions:
1. Belief – feeling or confidence that something is real, true or worthwhile especially in religious matters.
2. Values – any ideals, goals, standards on which actions or decisions are based.

Aims
1. To develop mature approaches to beliefs and disbeliefs.
2. To encourage conscious evaluation of values implicit in attitudes in and to particular situations.
3. To juxtapose R.E. and M.E. in such a way that pupils are encouraged to see contact points.
4. To promote tolerance in areas and subjects that generate heat!

Objectives and skills
1. To develop discussion and interaction skills.
2. To develop interview and cross-examination skills.
3. To communicate a basis of factual information.
4. To develop group, individual, class and larger-unit learning situations.
5. To develop written skills of self-expression.

Teaching methods
Compulsory general lessons can be a graveyard for teachers! They have to walk the tightrope between a carbon copy of formal exam-geared

78

work and, on the other side, the rest lesson where vague chat takes place until finally the pupils become bitterly resistant to any demand for written work. Sometimes such lessons are helped, sometimes undermined by a mixed-ability form-based approach; this is one thing we need to evaluate.

I think there are no easy solutions in this context, but there are some techniques we need to follow from the outset:

1. Attachment of one teacher to one class, preferably for the two year duration, but with lessons set across a half year so that lead lessons, visitors, outside visits, films can be shared without the isolation so often experienced by the general R.E. teacher.
2. As varied an approach as possible; film, filmstrip, video, outside speaker, group discussions, role play, class discussion, surveys, opinionnaire, formal written work, etc.

This in turn demands a certain commitment from the team:

1. Regular SHORT planning meetings, especially in the early stages of the course; post-lesson evaluation.
2. Division within the team, each taking responsibility for mounting part of the course, preparing the lesson that all will adapt to their own groups and, if necessary, gathering resources. It is also essential that someone co-ordinates the technical side, seeing that the projector, etc., is ready for the half-year population who are to view a programme.
3. The preparedness from the outset to pool any problems or issues.

SAMPLE SYLLABUS

Units

A quarter term per unit seems the ideal compromise to be fair to both the nature and depth of the topic and the length of pupil interest. The single lesson topic is too superficial to be of value.

Scheme

Year 4

Term 1
1. Traditional belief.
   (a) the power of beliefs (b) where beliefs come from (c) 'God talk'

79

(d) meet a believer (e) Church visits to R.C., C of E, Evangelical Baptist Churches (f) modern parables on film or soundstrip, for example 'The Stranger' or 'In the Bin' (Scripture Union).

2. Who am I?
3. The inner city in Derby with reference to Sikhism, including a half-day visit.
4. 'From our dog to your dog' (the British Christmas).

Term 2
5. What's a life worth?
   (a) abortion (b) euthanasia (c) the Holocaust (d) Chief Seattle's testimony.
6. What every Westerner needs to know about Islam.
7. The future.
8. Quakerism *or* Hinduism.

Term 3
9. Punishment: theory; practice; what do our attitudes reveal about us?
10. Commitment to a belief.
11. Honesty.
12. The Outsider in society and religion; tolerance.

Term 4
13. Education: what's it for?; religious education.
14. Holy books (Bible, Quran, Granth Sahib, *Science & Health*, Book of Mormon: attitudes and interpretation).
15. Death and after life (attitudes; post–death experience; reincarnation; Jesus; heaven and hell).
16. Race.

Term 5
17. Crisis (Samaritans, Marriage Guidance).
18. Quakerism *or* Hinduism (whichever was omitted in Term 2).
19. 'R.E. TV' A video interview: subject, content, 'personalities', production by the group.
20. The numinous.

Term 6
21. Me, my world, my beliefs (Aims and ambitions, introduced by filmstrips, e.g. "Enry' and 'Writing on the Wall', issued by Scripture Union).

ALTERNATIVE FOURTH/FIFTH YEAR NON-EXAMINATION RE COURSE

1 *Being a Christian*
Dimensions:
  belief
  worship
  behaviour
  attitudes to the Bible

2 *Being a humanist*
Dimensions:
  belief
  behaviour
  humanist organisations

3 *Being an agnostic or atheist*
Dimensions:
  reasons for unbelief
  morality without religion

4 *Being 'on the fringe'*
Dimensions:
  the psychic; the numinous; yoga, TM etc; folk religion

5 *Being religious in an indifferent environment*
Case study: Sikhism in Derby

6 *Attitudes to death and after-life*

Notes:
This syllabus is planned for a school in an area in which Christianity is the only effective religious option. A non-examination course cannot justify an academic study in years Four and Five of world faiths as ends in themselves unless they are living in the school or its catchment. The

breakdown here into six units does not imply that these should be treated at equal length, but they do explore the real options open to pupils in the environment I have described.

A *Factual Information*
1. Jesus was by religion (a) Jewish (b) Hebrew (c) Christian.
2. In their attitude to abortion Christians are (a) for (b) against (c) divided.
3. The Holy Shroud is damaged by (a) mishandling (b) fire (c) water (d) fire and water (e) vandalism.
4. In general Christian belief is (a) uniform (they think the same) (b) vague (they don't know) (c) diverse (they vary).
5. The word evangelical means (a) Baptist (b) bringing Good News (c) anti R.C.
6. Muslims believe Allah is (a) One (b) Three (c) Muhammad.
7. Muslims believe the Quran is (a) like the Bible (b) a useful book (c) almost dictated by God.
8. Ramadan is (a) a fast (b) a mosque tower (c) a pointer to Mecca (d) a pulpit.
9. Hinduism takes its name from (a) India (b) Hindus (c) the Indus river (d) Benares (e) Krishna.
10. Quakers describe themselves as (a) the Peace Church (b) Fox's People (c) Society of Friends (d) Seekers.

B *Weighing Evidence*
11. If the Shroud is genuine it would prove (a) nothing (b) that Jesus was crucified (c) that Jesus rose from the dead.
12. Symbols in the parish church are meant (a) to look decorative (b) to point to a reality beyond (c) to give worshippers some distraction.
13. Quakers would object most to (a) communion services (b) war (c) other churches (d) being laughed at.
14. Punishment to most Christians should be (a) to deter (b) to reform (c) retribution.
15. A Samaritan should (a) give you advice (b) help to solve your own problems (c) help neighbours.

16. Muslims would object to being called Mohammedans.
17. Girls of 10 were once hanged in England.
18. Chief Seattle foresaw modern problems, e.g., pollution.
19. 'In the Bin' is about the badges we put on each other.
20. Leonard Arthur was found guilty of attempted murder.

D *Course Assessment*
21. Name the unit you found most interesting.
22. Name the unit you found least interesting.
23. Which teaching method did you most enjoy?
    (class/lesson/filmstrip/video/speaker/outside visit/discussion).
24. List ONE important thing you have learnt in R.E. this year.
25. Is there any way in which your own attitude to religion has changed this year?

E *Arguing the Case*
26. List 3 arguments *for* abortion.
27. List 3 arguments *against* capital punishment.
28. List 2 reasons *for* belief in God.
29. List 2 reasons *against* euthanasia (mercy killing).

F *Choose the Most Mature Statement* (whether or not you agree with it)
30. (a) God is rubbish (b) when you look at suffering God is hard to believe in (c) God cannot possibly exist.
31. (a) Religion is one area of human experience
    (b) Religion is a waste of time
    (c) Religion is dead.
32. (a) All religions are obviously wrong.
    (b) All religions are obviously right.
    (c) All religions are obviously different.
33. (a) Please God, give me a bike.
    (b) Send me a miracle, God.
    (c) Let your will be done, God.
34. Father Christmas is (a) a children's fantasy (b) a powerful idea (c) a silly old man.

35. The video about the future (a) was a comedy about a grandfather (b) was a scientific study (c) was about a breakdown of the family.
36. An outsider (a) is rejected by others (b) rejects others (c) might be (a) and (b).
37. Honesty is (a) not stealing money (b) not lying (c) looking at your own life truthfully.
38. To a Hindu good and bad (a) both come from God (Brahman) (b) come from God and the Devil (c) are unimportant.
39. The aim of R.E. should be (a) to make people Christian (b) to make people religious (c) to help people to think out their own beliefs and disbeliefs.

GENERAL R.E. END OF COURSE SELF ASSESSMENT

Name   Form
This is designed to help you to assess FACTS you've learned, SKILLS you've used and ATTITUDES you've developed or changed.

Facts
Answer in a word or phrase
 1 The central piece of furniture in a parish church is
 2 The Bin Man in 'In the Bin' might represent
 3 Seattle asked 'How can you buy . . . . . .?'
 4 The Muslim name for God is
 5 The most regular religious act of all Muslims is
 6 Quakers believe that inside all people is something of
 7 The holy book originally (allegedly) written on gold plates is
 8 The proper name for the Hindu cycle of rebirth is
 9 One biblical book, used at funerals, that speaks of God wiping away tears is
10 Numinous means
11 The South African Church that supports apartheid is
12 One example of a caucasoid race is
13 The 'Final Solution' was
14 Punishment intended to put you off wrongdoing is called
15 The Holy Shroud is now kept in

Skills

16, 17 List one argument for, one against euthanasia.

18 What skill(s) is involved in doing that?

19 The unit 'From our dog to your dog' was really about . . .

20 Distinguish between prejudice and discrimination.

21 Strictly, the only answer to 'Do you believe in God?' is 'It depends on . . . .'

22 The game *Logikon* is designed to get pupils to think about . . .

23 A class debate in R.E. will expose some prejudices ('I hate whites'), some beliefs ('Jesus rose') and some skills. List THREE skills.

24 Name one drawback of video as a teaching method.

Attitude

Sometimes pupils feel a school report is unfair. Try as honestly as you can to assess yourself on the following scale for each question 'V.Good Good Average Below Average Poor'. Then check it with your teacher's opinion.

25 What sort of listener am I in class?

26 How have I performed on worksheets?

27 What oral contribution have I made?

28 What has been my attitude to non-exam work in general?

29 Rate your tolerance of others' views.

It is said of many things that what you get out of the activity depends on what you put into it:

30 Is this TRUE/FALSE of this course?

During this course you have grown two years and (theoretically) matured. Name any way in which your attitude to any issue on this course has changed.

OR

Name any topic you wish the course had covered which it hasn't.

Acknowledgements

Books do not write themselves, nor do authors give birth to them without an attendant team of midwives. I have been fortunate in mine: Alan Brown and Allan Lancashire both read the manuscript at an early stage and gave advice from their R.E. and Church education expertise;

Peter Doble and David Sellick readily agreed to permission to quote an extract from *In the Beginning*, a report I edited by and for probationers, in which David Sellick wrote on resources and the York R.E. Centre published;

Mr Moss of Moss Office Services Ltd of Belper, through his typist Mr Hough, prepared a final typescript in record time and well copied;

Pamela Egan and Barbara England provided advice and publishing expertise, while Michael Proctor provided the title in after-lunch quip.

To all these, and others, a big thank you.